BETTER than OK

HELPING YOUNG PEOPLE TO FLOURISH AT SCHOOL AND BEYOND

EDITED BY DR HELEN STREET AND NEIL PORTER

FREMANTLE PRESS

ACKNOWLEDGEMENTS

Neil and I have felt part of a truly inspirational team during the creation of this very precious book. Our heartfelt thanks go to all of the authors who have so wisely and generously contributed to the chapters presented here. Each of you continues to make an incredibly valuable contribution to youth mental health and wellbeing in Australia and internationally. Thank you for sharing your thoughts and ideas here, for joining us in the ongoing creation of Positive Schools, and for your continued work in this area. We have learnt so much professionally from each of you, and delighted in the added bonus of making some very dear friends in the process.

Second, an enormous thank you to the wonderful and wise Jane Fraser at Fremantle Press. Jane, you not only embraced this project wholeheartedly, you did so knowing we were aiming to meet the craziest of crazy deadlines. Your faith in us ensured we produced not only a great book, but a great book on time. Thank you also to others at Fremantle Press who supported our journey with such enthusiasm and expertise. In particular, we would like to thank Claire Miller for bringing her business skills to the fore.

Next, a very special thank you to Janet Blagg for editing so many diverse and varied chapters with such mindfulness, skill and sensitivity. Janet, you have managed to support each author with their own distinct voice while always ensuring the chapters flow together towards the same aims and ideals. You have been a pleasure to work with.

Neil and I would also like to take this opportunity to express our ongoing and immense gratitude to all of the people who have made and continue to make the Positive Schools conferences such a success. Those behind the scenes, on the stage and in the audience. The Positive Schools conferences have not only been the main inspiration for this book, they have provided a firm foundation for its conception and delivery.

Finally, a very loving thank you to Lucia, Molly and Tess for providing a very personal reason for Neil and me to be advocates of youth wellbeing, for lighting up our lives every day and for ensuring that we too strive to be better than OK.

Helen Street

CONTENTS

Embracing True Identities

Practising Positive Relationships

Growing Up in Nurturing Environments

Living with Technology

Flourishing at School

INTRODUCTION
POSITIVE SCHOOLS,
POSITIVE TALK
DR HELEN STREET

Wellbeing is the basis of flourishing, which is the ultimate expression of being well. This is a book about helping young people to flourish – at home, at school and in life.

Flourishing is a term that describes someone who is confident in their identity, assertive in their social interactions, loving towards themselves and others, resilient to life's inevitable setbacks and engaged in activities that embrace their strengths and passions. Kids who flourish have the greatest potential of all because they have the potential to be happy. Kids who flourish are kids who experience wellbeing and apply that wellbeing to living their lives in a positive and healthy way.

Nearly all parents want, above all else, for their children to flourish in life, to be happy and live their lives accordingly. Still, there remains a wide difference of opinion about the role of the education system in supporting flourishing as a primary aim. Some educators embrace social and emotional learning; others suggest that while social and emotional competency may be important, education is primarily an academic pursuit. It seems to me that this debate is redundant in the light of a growing body of research telling us that academic potential is most successfully fulfilled in the presence of wellbeing. In fact, just about anything we do in life is done more successfully, more passionately and with greater love and commitment, when done in the presence of wellbeing.

Young people make healthier and more positive choices about their current and future learning when they are happy and well. And they are more likely to develop social competency when they have a firm foundation of wellbeing from which to launch themselves into a social world. As such, wellbeing is a vital beginning as much as it is an ultimate desire. Wellbeing is the basis of flourishing. Flourishing is the ultimate expression of being well.

The really good news about all this lies in the knowledge that every child and teen has the potential to flourish in life. No matter where an individual's strengths lie or where they are placed among the social and academic milieu, they can flourish as people. Although it is indeed true that some of us are born with greater vulnerability or sensitivity than others, none of us is born anxious or depressed. None of us is born without hope or a desire to embrace life.

Not everyone will be deemed 'good' at what they do, or be made rich in consequence. Some of us are born into undeniable hardship, conflict and poverty. However, it is our connection with living that measures life success, not some absolute level of achievement. Some kids are born with a natural leaning towards academic pursuits, others with a passion for the arts or a love of sport or creative thinking. No-one is born without the potential to find passion and engagement in some aspect of life. In short, everyone is born with the potential to flourish, to be happy and live well, if only they are given the opportunity to do so.

It is time we stopped measuring the success of our children based upon their comparative performance against their peers or some arbitrary outcome. While only a few may excel in our material world, we all have the opportunity to engage in life.

Twenty-seven authors have contributed to the thirty-two chapters presented here, each exceptional in their own right as advocates for youth mental health and wellbeing. Each has also contributed in the Australian Positive Schools conferences, the source of inspiration for this book.

The Positive Schools conferences started in Western Australia (WA) in 2009. They came about after Neil Porter and I decided there was a real need to help teachers embrace well-researched concrete strategies to support wellbeing in their schools and colleges. We wanted a conference that eschewed graphs, psychobabble and statistics and focused instead on grounded, practical and sustainable solutions. Positive Schools was launched as a one-day event with the support of the Graduate School of Education at the University of Western Australia (UWA). This first conference featured an inspirational keynote address by burns specialist Professor Fiona Wood and contributions from inspirational speakers like George W. Burns. When all 250 places were taken up two months beforehand, we knew we were engaging in something important.

The following year, iconic leader in anti-racism Jane Elliott flew in from the US for our two-day event. The day she arrived, Neil and I met her for coffee. We brought cookies, our third child, still a baby, and our barely restrained excitement. Jane's warmth, wit and intelligence made our conversation a joy. After two hours she asked about the purpose of our discussion, presuming we needed to talk about the practicalities of the next few days. 'Oh, no,' we exclaimed, 'we simply wanted to meet you.' Since that first coffee, Jane has been an ongoing advocate of Positive Schools. Her chapter 'On Education' describes the personal lesson she learnt from her historic 'Blue Eyes/Brown Eyes' exercise.

By 2011 our confidence had grown along with our reputation, and we welcomed a new member of the team, Richard Pengelley. We decided to present a conference in Brisbane, along with a three-day event in WA. The WA conference featured a day for parents in recognition of their investment in their children's futures. Five presenters, including myself, gave talks to over 300 dedicated mums and dads.

We established ourselves at the Esplanade Hotel in Fremantle where we could accommodate our growing numbers. Our event featured the lovable Steve Biddulph along with the most passionate advocate for youth wellbeing I have met, Dr Michael Carr-Gregg. Michael also spoke in Queensland at our special bullying themed Positive Schools, hosted by the ABC's Tony Jones. Michael has since become a Positive Schools ambassador and a regular and highly valued member of the team. We were also graced by the wise words of Donna Cross and Toni Noble in 2011, and I am proud to say that both these highly respected women have become Positive Schools ambassadors since that time.

In 2012 we ran three events (in WA, Queensland and Victoria), all featuring a masterclass on sexuality. Along with our main conference day and multiple workshops, Sandra Sully from Australia's Channel Ten hosted a full day of discussion that included contributions from Melinda Tankard Reist and Holly Brennan. Peak national bodies for wellbeing – KidsMatter, MindMatters and beyondblue – joined us as conference partners, as well as providing popular workshops. They remain key supporters to this day.

In 2013 the most successful and uplifting Positive Schools to date was again held in the three states. The ABC's Kerry O'Brien hosted a masterclass on engaging students at school. I spent an incredible three weeks presenting alongside Michael Carr-Gregg, 'Dr Happy' aka Tim Sharp, Andrew Martin and Jason Clarke on the second day of each event. The entertaining and informed voices of Andrew Fuller and Maggie Dent welcomed a full house in all three states on day one of each event. In addition, Geelong Grammar School joined the team as a key conference partner and this was happily reflected in a clear focus on Positive Education.

In 2014 Neil and I are excited to be introducing the inaugural Sydney conference, so that Positive Schools will be represented in four states. We are partnering with Google along with the Alannah and Madeline Foundation and the Young and Well Cooperative Research Centre to present a packed event embracing creativity and technology. In addition, our established partners, beyondblue, KidsMatter, MindMatters and Geelong Grammar School, all continue to offer their support and enthusiasm. In 2014 we feature a wide range of speakers including the warm and insightful Andrew Fiu.

In this book we travel from moving and uplifting stories to well-researched theories and back again. Each chapter stands distinct in terms of style and content. Yet all have unifying and inspiring themes in common, based on the belief that parents and teachers have the power and responsibility to help young people to flourish, and that flourishing is possible for all.

Andrew Fiu observes in our opening chapter that as adults we spend many thousands of hours caring for our kids. Time can sometimes seem endless, sometimes far too brief. It is always precious.

What can we do to help young people use their own time in a positive, passionate and meaningful way? How can we help them to flourish? To be better than OK?

ENGAGING WITH LIFE

KEEPING TIME WITH THE GATEKEEPERS
ANDREW FIU

Today is a challenging time no matter how you look at it and there is the rub. Time. You have several thousand hours to influence and inspire kids. How will you spend it?

According to the Australian Organisation of Economic Co-operation and Development (OECD), students receive an average of 7751 hours of instruction during their primary and lower secondary education, most of it compulsory. Around 51 per cent of those hours are spent learning reading, writing, literature and mathematics, taught primarily by teachers who are forty years of age or older in an average classroom size of 25 in a school system ill equipped to keep up with rapid technological advances.

In 1996, a research study by Joan Middendorf and Alan Kalish of Indiana University reported on students' attention spans in classrooms and lectures. It seems the average mind shuts down after between six and twenty minutes – irrespective of the teacher, how interesting the subject matter is, the time of day or the environment the teaching is taking place in.

When we were growing up the teacher was the 'gatekeeper' to all knowledge and information. Today, search engines are progressively taking up that role. Anybody can learn calculus or how to build a tree house or design an app on the internet. We need to be more assertive, more creative, and we need to think differently because the traditional approach is not working in a world where students have smartphones and tablets, interact via social media and texting, and find answers by googling.

Technological advances are transforming the needs of the labour market and impacting on low-skilled workers who are increasingly finding their traditional jobs being automated. A tertiary education increases the likelihood of being employed, and the higher the educational achievement, the larger the pay packet. In New Zealand, a year after graduation, students who had majored in health and engineering received salaries that were on average 58 and 45 per cent more respectively than those who graduated in the creative arts (OECD, 2013). The question is, how to influence students to stay longer in school in a world where they don't see that what they're learning is relevant to what they'll be doing when they start working, some of them in jobs that don't even yet exist.

Since 2006, I have toured colleges and universities where I discuss creative writing and the evolution of finding one's own creative groove. I have sat alongside students who have studied my book and spoken with teachers about why some techniques work and others do not when engaging students, particularly those from the lower socioeconomic groups.

I am not a teacher. I didn't pursue higher education, not because I didn't want to go to university but because after spending long bouts in hospital, I didn't qualify. In the early 1980s, schooling in hospitals was almost non-existent for long-term patients of school age. But something happened that helped ignite a love of reading and learning – I heard the stories of elderly patients who shared my room. I was captivated by their tales of travels and adventures, of hopeful dreams in faraway lands and the disappointment of colourful mistakes. It didn't matter that I was the only brown kid in a predominantly European ward or that I was the youngest at fourteen years old. It was my education, a series of daily events that were really discussions and conversations. It could be one to one or a group of four or five. Occasionally up to ten patients would cram a hallway to discuss everything from politics and world wars to gardening and farming techniques; the best way to cook a roast dinner, navigating the Atlantic by the stars or arguing the voice patterns of pre-1960 singers of Cole Porter songs.

It was only later I realised how important these moments were and how they had armed me with an understanding my peers knew nothing about. I didn't have a highflying sixth form certificate and I didn't possess a University Entrance Certificate, but I knew I had valuable knowledge. I asked different questions, my interests were wider than what was discussed at school. I had a different type of knowledge after spending almost two years in and out of hospital.

A teacher once asked me to define 'knowledge' when I was trying to describe my lacklustre interest in Shakespeare. Words failed me because I didn't know how to structure a good response, and I was viewed as distinctly ignorant – the total opposite of knowledgeable. Inside I knew my elderly friends would have parodied the play, taken on the roles, and made me the lead character. They would have chastised me for not taking it seriously and helped me create a scene in the castles Shakespeare was so fond of. They would have roped in a passing orderly to play a guard and a nurse to play a cook, all the while explaining, questioning me, even beseeching me to respond as if I had been wronged by some crazy king. If I'd known what I know now, I would have said to the teacher that knowledge comes not just from reading a book but from instilling in me a desire to want to explore, to be open to learning. Because when I'm alone with my own thoughts, I'll still be questioning, still be excited about the subject and wanting to learn more.

I love both teachers and parents for what they do. Theirs is an often thankless task: to nurture and mould young minds and prepare them with a solid base from which to launch themselves into a future, equipped to achieve their dreams and expectations. It is a herculean duty and the responsibility to influence one mind let alone hundreds over the years is immense. Today is a challenging time no matter how you look at it and there is the rub. Time. You have several thousand hours to influence and inspire kids. How will you spend it? With great duty comes great opportunity.

Middendorf, J. & Kalish, A. (1996). *National Teaching & Learning Forum Journal, 5(2)*, pp. 1–12.

OECD (2013). *Education at a Glance 2013: OECD Indicators*, OECD Publishing (www.dx.doi.org/10.1787/eag-2013-en).

Find out more about Andrew and his book *Purple Heart* by visiting his website (www.lifeafter6.com).

PERSONAL BEST GOALS AND STUDENT GROWTH

PROFESSOR ANDREW J. MARTIN

In an era of national testing, school league tables and competition, there are the beginnings of a shift towards greater recognition of students' personal academic growth. Personal Best (PB) goals are an effective way in which to encourage young learners to aim higher.

In an era of national literacy and numeracy testing, school league tables, heightened performance pressure and classroom competition, there are the beginnings of a shift towards greater recognition of students' personal academic growth. Increasingly, educators and researchers are growing uncomfortable with the excessive focus on comparisons and competition in the classroom. They fear it locks too many students out of opportunities for success, places too much pressure on students at all levels of ability in the classroom, and increases anxiety and fear of failure. This has led to calls for a focus on students' personal academic growth alongside the more traditional comparative approaches, in the belief that it will give all young people greater access to success (in terms of personal improvement) and reduce anxiety and fear of failure.

Comparisons and competition are a reality of today's world, and in this chapter I will show how you can complement these with personal best (PB) and growth approaches.

PB goals are an effective way to encourage young learners to aim higher by competing with themselves more than competing with other students. PB goals are specific, challenging and completely self-referenced. In setting a PB goal, you encourage a student to state exactly what they are aiming for, and set a goal which moves them forward and that competes primarily with previous bests rather than with other students.

Process and outcome goals

PB goals may be either *process* or *outcome* goals. Both should be encouraged.

Process goals
- reading one more book for the present assignment than on the previous assignment
- preparing for a test at the weekend when previously no study had been done at weekends
- doing some homework that night when none had been done that week
- aiming to be less anxious in the upcoming test than in the previous test
- calling out in class fewer times today than yesterday
- staying in one's seat longer in the afternoon than in the morning
- asking a teacher for help when previously the teacher was avoided
- spending an extra hour doing homework than usual.

Outcome goals
- spelling more words in this week's spelling quiz than last week's quiz
- doing better on the term 2 science practical report than on the term 1 report
- scoring a higher GPA in semester 2 than semester 1
- getting a higher mark in the end of year exams than in the half yearly exams
- getting more sums correct in this week's mathematics test than last week's test.

There is good evidence demonstrating the effectiveness of PB goals. Our research program has found PB goals to be associated with positive educational aspirations, enjoyment of school, class participation and persistence. PB goals lead to literacy and numeracy achievement, test effort and homework completion; they are associated with deep learning, academic flow and positive teacher relationships. This effectiveness applies equally to students who are at academic risk, such as those with ADHD.

Ten steps to PB goal setting

1. Clearly understand what a PB goal is.
2. Observe sample PB goals to get a better idea of different types of goals.
3. Decide whether to pursue a process or an outcome goal.
4. Precisely state what the PB goal is.
5. Ensure the PB goal is at least matching a previous best and that it is realistic and attainable.
6. Specify a timeframe for reaching the PB goal.
7. List the steps involved in working towards the PB goal.
8. Monitor progress on these steps.
9. Reflect on whether the goal has been achieved, and if it was not attained, identify the reasons why.
10. Set the next PB goal.

The PB Index

The PB Index is an informal approach to scoring students in a way that indicates how well they are performing from one term to the next. You score the student on three areas based on how the student has travelled in this term compared to last term:

- This term's mark compared to last term's mark.
- This term's engagement and attitude compared to last term's.
- This term's skill and competence development compared to last term's.

A higher score reflects how much the student has exceeded their efforts from the previous term, and the three scores are summed to form a total PB Index for the term. The PB Index can be included in the student's report card alongside their comparative grade to give a more comprehensive reading. The comparative grade reveals how students performed compared to the class and the PB Index shows how much they achieved relative to their own potential.

Learning growth maps

Too often students have no concept of what progress they are making as they move through a given topic or unit of work. Learning growth maps are helpful in this regard. For example, prior to embarking on the fractions unit in mathematics, you might identify the different parts of the topic that students will progressively learn: proper fractions followed by improper fractions, then adding proper fractions, multiplying them, and so on. This is referred to as mapping learning growth. As a student learns each part, they check that off on their learning growth map, and so have a sense of their progress.

Growth feed-forward

Another approach to growth is through the feedback you provide students on their assignments and projects. Often feedback by teachers is summative; it mainly comments on the strengths and weaknesses of the work, along with various corrections. Such feedback does not typically address the student's potential for growth, with advice on what they can do to improve in future efforts. In contrast, growth 'feed-forward' is forward reaching, identifying errors in terms of what students can do to improve next time. This 'feed-forward' is very specific and launches a young person into more successful practice in a subsequent task.

The growth mindset

Underpinning these specific strategies are various mindsets students can have about themselves, their ability and potential. Holding an 'incremental view' (growth mindset), students believe that their competence and skill can be developed through effort and a positive attitude, and that they have the room and potential to grow academically. Holding an 'entity view,' students do not believe that competence and skill can be developed much, even if good effort and attitude are applied, and they see themselves as somewhat stuck at where they are. Your task is to promote a growth mindset and reduce entity views of ability and potential. What more can we ask of students than to aim to improve on their own previous efforts – and believe it is possible?

....

Dweck, C.S. (2006). *Mindset: The new psychology of success*. New York, Random House.

Martin, A.J. (2010). *Building classroom success: Eliminating academic fear and failure*. London, Continuum.

Martin, A.J. (2011). 'Personal best (PB) approaches to academic development: Implications for motivation and assessment'. *Educational Practice and Theory, 33*, pp. 93–9.

Martin, A.J. (2012). *Academic Growth Framework – Worksheets for Educators, Parents, and Students*. Sydney, Lifelong Achievement Group (www.lifelongachievement.com).

Martin, A.J. (2013). 'The Personal Proficiency Network: Key self-system factors and processes to optimize academic development'. In D.M. McInerney, H.W. Marsh., R.G. Craven, & F. Guay (eds). *Theory driving research: New wave perspectives on self-processes and human development*. Charlotte, NC, Information Age Publishing.

Visit www.lifelongachievement.com to download Andrew's worksheets and more information about personal bests.

FROM REACTION TO CREATION
DR HELEN STREET

Our creativity is an essential element of our wellbeing.
We need to learn to express ourselves in the artefacts
of our world so that we can feel a part of that world.
Creativity is not a luxury. Young people need to be
creative to be well.

I have noticed that we often put the word 'creative' alongside the word 'genius' when describing an innovative or artistic achievement. Similarly we often talk about expressions of creativity as if they stem from exceptional talent or highly intelligent minds. In this way of thinking, creativity is seen as a luxury for the masses and an expression reserved for the few. It seems the rest of us need to settle for the passive appreciation of creativity rather than the active creation of the world around us. Yet creativity is not a talent born to a lucky few, it is an innate element of being human, a part of every one of us. Just as we all can learn literacy and numeracy, so too can we learn to nurture and express our creativity.

Our creativity is an essential element of our wellbeing. Not only do we all have the capacity to respond creatively (rather than simply reactively) to the world around us, we *need* to be creative to feel 'wholly' human. We need to learn to express ourselves in the artefacts of our world so that we can feel a part of that world. It is of little surprise to find that whenever I ask another adult to tell me the thing they would 'really like to do' if money and time and opportunity were no object, they nearly always answer with a creative pursuit. Lawyers have told me they would like to be artists; engineers express a love for singing and IT experts want to write 'that' book. This is not to say that each of these professionals could not find creativity in what they currently do, but rather that engaging with something wholeheartedly creative is a genuine desire for most people.

In a society that must deal with challenging and prevalent mental health issues in kids and teens, the pursuit of creativity may seem a luxury or out of touch with the 'real world.' Yet the active pursuit of creativity has been found to significantly improve wellbeing in young people. Moreover, it has been found to help them to be 'better than OK,' to flourish and feel more content, more satisfied with life as a whole. Creative expression is a valuable and vital form of expression, whether it be in verbal or written language, the language of science or math, or the language of art or music. It is time that we understood that creativity is essential, not the folly of the rich or an exclusive gift for the chosen few.

So how do we support creativity in young people in a modern world where they are so busy being instantly entertained with screen time and social media? And how do we help them to prioritise creativity when the demands of school assessments seem oblivious to it?

First, we need to ensure that creativity is rid of its mystical and elusive standing. It needs to be considered essential to more than the preschooler eager to draw the next picture. As Picasso so beautifully said, 'all children are artists, the problem is how to remain an artist once he grows up.' One of the most fundamental ways to help kids find and develop creativity is to stop bringing them up to be purely reactive, passive voyeurs in a world of easy entertainment. We need to help them to be bored.

How often, as parents and educators, we hear the words, 'I'm bored!' Or, 'I can't think of anything to do.' All too often children asked to come up with an activity or an idea will falter within a matter of minutes. But rather than believe boredom is a problem state to be in, it is time we revisited the true value of being bored as a necessary step in any creative process.

'I have no idea what to do,' is a statement designed to fill adults with anxiety and spur us into action to rescue our frustrated children. In today's world the idea of boredom is associated with the idea of teachers and parents abandoning their children's needs, being inadequate providers of 'interesting things to do' or simply being unable to keep up with the short attention span of a younger person.

Our children know this all too well. They triumphantly announce boredom as a means to be given permission to change activities, be given access to easy entertainment or extra adult attention to solve the problem.

I often counter expressions of boredom with a suggestion that my children help with the housework or other chores. Looks of horror arise in response. When I suggest other solutions such as 'go play with your sisters,' or, 'why don't you read a book,' I am generally met with disdain, as if I just don't get it. It seems that being bored means being uninterested in doing much at all. In contrast, on the rare occasions when I allow TV or a movie as a solution, my children's eyes light up as they reach for the remote control. Being bored equates with a desire to be passively, reactively entertained.

In recent years I have spent most of my professional time becoming increasingly absorbed with the joy of running the Positive Schools conferences. A major theme of the 2014 events is technology and mental health, and my attention has been turned to the double-edged role of technology in both supporting youth wellbeing and creating mental health issues. The theme of creativity complements these ideas well, and asks whether technology is promoting or hindering creativity in young people. It is this question that leads me to revisit current thinking about the concept of boredom in our technologically driven society.

Increasing access to modern technology provides us with numerous avenues for easy, passive entertainment in addition to numerous ways to communicate with others in an informal way. No longer do I have to stare into space while waiting at the check-out: I can check my phone messages, text messages, email, Facebook or Twitter. At home I can turn on the TV anytime, browse on Google or pick up my iPad for a whole entertainment system on my lap. How easy it is 'not to be bored.'

My husband and I limit our children's amount of screen time, since they too have learnt that the wonders of technology can stave off boredom with very little effort.

Home-based technology offers a means for all sorts of creative pursuits, but too often it is used only for passive entertainment. The many options available may stop the immediate cries of boredom, but they also stop kids actively seeking out purposeful, creative activities. If you never have to amuse yourself or develop your own ideas or passions, then over the long term you will never learn to be self-reliant or self-directed in your behaviour. Passive entertainment is only ever a bandaid for the absence of self-determined action.

Thus, one of the biggest problems of access to passive entertainment at the tap of a screen is the dampening of self-directed and intrinsically motivated activities. Without these, creativity is also constrained. With the instant appeal of technological entertainment we might start to believe that we don't have to be concerned with being creative or 'suffer' the frustration of being bored. Yet creativity is a vital element in life and boredom a vital step in the journey. Having time to be bored means having time to develop creatively. Ultimately, anything becomes boring if we are not actively engaged in it.

If I am strong enough to ignore the cries of Sunday afternoon boredom from my children, I can guarantee that they will creatively and happily be involved in an activity within twenty minutes. Once they have stopped fretting about not being entertained by something or someone else, they begin to focus on what they *can* do for themselves; what they *can* create. When you are used to instant entertainment, twenty minutes can seem a long time, however a self-directed creative pursuit may go on to engage a child for a whole day, a week or even a lifetime.

Many great ideas have stemmed from having the opportunity to actually think about things, or, indeed, to think about nothing at all. If we are constantly structuring our attention with the passive process of gazing at a screen, we are not giving ourselves the opportunity to actively seek out our passions in life or to develop creative ideas of our own.

If children are not used to addressing the benefits of boredom, then begin with easy steps. Guide them to some suggestions for age-appropriate activities. Offer lots of support and encouragement for ventures that stem out of boredom. As kids become better at being self-directed learners, the time taken to 'stop being bored' will decrease. And as creative skills develop, the level of creativity achieved will increase. It can seem a brave and almost radical move to allow kids to be bored, stuck without an idea. We can start by keeping a check on our own impatient, technologically driven selves and not rushing in to save them too soon.

Next time a child lets you know that they are horrendously bored, cheer in celebration and let them know that this means they are going to create something wonderful very soon. Redefine boredom as a positive step in every creative learning process, as a means to positive self-development and enhanced wellbeing. How brilliant it is to be bored. How necessary it is that we move from reaction to creation.

....

To find out more about Helen's work and to read a wide range of articles she has written visit her website (www.helenstreet.com.au).

FINDING MOTIVATION

JOSH'S STORY
DAN HAESLER

To what extent does knowing what you are or are not good at shape your life? How have your life's experiences and ambitions been shaped by your abilities? For most of us, our school experiences go a long way to shaping our identity.

'You'll struggle getting anything out of this one,' the handwritten note said. It came at the bottom of a set of notes compiled by Josh's Year 6 teachers at a local primary school.

I was fresh out of university in my first 'real' teaching job in the UK. As is often the way with a new teacher, I was given a Year 7 class to tutor. This is a kind of home-room scenario in which the tutor remains with the group throughout their school career. Tutoring involved delivering a prescribed program that incorporated things like goal setting and organisational skills and generally being the first point of contact in the school if students got into trouble.

Most of the boys in my Year 7 group had been identified as cheeky at best, and downright troublesome at worst. Their primary schools seemed to be happy to be rid of them, although the majority of teachers indicated that the boys had the potential to do well academically, they just needed to be engaged. All the boys had shown themselves keen to learn, at least occasionally, with the exception of Josh.

I hate to admit it now, but fresh to the teaching game, I took the teachers' notes on face value and figured Josh would end up finding his own way out of school into an apprenticeship or something else suitable. School just wasn't for him, right? We all know kids like that. As a new teacher I was ill equipped to provide Josh with any strategies to improve other than to offer an encouraging comment or sympathetic ear every now and then.

Josh meandered through Years 7 and 8 getting Ds. Teachers questioned his attitude, though he was rarely in trouble for anything more than not handing in work – until a couple of weeks before the end of Year 8, when I got a phone call asking me to come and remove Josh from class. He'd told his teacher to '*f— off!*' and was becoming aggressive towards anyone trying to calm him down.

I walked in and asked him to come with me. We'd developed a pretty good relationship to this point, so he came outside knowing I'd at least hear him out. We sat in the playground until he had calmed down, then I asked him what was wrong. It turned out Josh had attempted to answer a question in class and got it horribly wrong, at which the whole class burst into laughter.

'I'm shit at everything sir,' Josh said, then apologised for swearing. 'Everyone tells me, my teachers, my mum and now my mates!'

I asked him what he meant by *everything* and he said, 'Maths, English, Science, y'know *everything.*'

Really? *That's everything?* I asked him what he *was* good at.

'Nothing,' he replied, and then, 'at school anyway, and that's all anyone cares about, innit?'

It turned out that Josh was really interested in – if not good at – cooking, photography and street art. He had developed his cooking skills through necessity as his mum worked two jobs and he would cook for his younger siblings, but now he was starting to come up with his own recipes.

His interest in photography predated today's teen obsessions for posting 'selfies' to Facebook. Josh was using his grandad's old SLR camera to take shots of everyday life in the streets around him, as well as examples of street art that he found exciting.

I asked whether he enjoyed Home Economics or Art at school.

'Nah sir, the teachers don't like me, and anyway, they're girls' subjects, innit?'

We laughed, but it did highlight a big problem. Josh *should* have enjoyed Home Economics or Art at school, but he didn't. Throughout his time at primary school he had developed the belief he was 'dumb' and 'no good at anything.' When he did try, he failed. So he decided it was better not to try in the first place. Better to get into trouble for not doing work than get called dumb. The less he tried, the less he progressed. And so it became a self-fulfilling prophecy.

We talked about this for a while, and I urged him to think more of himself than just the grades he received on his report card.

Intelligence – being smart, clever or good at something – comes in many guises, but society tends to value the academic guises more than others. And this has a great deal to do with how we educate our kids.

Think about yourself for a minute. Are *you* good at maths? What about drawing? Or singing? How old were you when you decided whether you were any good or not? To what extent does knowing what you are or are not good at shape your life? How have your life's experiences and ambitions been shaped by your abilities? For many of us, our school experience goes a long way to help shape our identity – particularly with regard to what we can or can't do. It also impacts on how we see others.

Consider your own family. Who are the musicians? Who are the mathematicians? Who are the sport stars in your genetic pool? You can probably categorise your family members pretty easily. I'll bet you can also name those who you wouldn't bother calling if you were putting together a pub trivia team, or if your soccer team was a player short. We don't do this to be unkind or to exclude anyone, it's just that, 'Oh well, you know, she's not all that sporty,' or, 'He's better with his hands than he is with his head.' We categorise or label people because it's easy, convenient, and we tell ourselves it's a necessary thing to do.

Think of your own kids for a minute. Even allowing for the standard-issue, rose-tinted glasses that you received in the birthing suite, I'm sure your kids do things that amaze you on a daily basis. However, what we consider worthy of praise changes significantly as our children grow up. So while their ability to feed themselves at age two gets a daily Facebook update with pictures, by the time they turn five, it's a different story.

As our children develop, the variety of things we praise decreases, but the weight of praise we attach to an achievement or talent *increases*, especially if their abilities are recognised with something tangible, like kindergarten *Student of the Week* certificates or car bumper stickers. Most schools operate a rewards-based program, from the humble certificate through to the car sticker, with some schools now bestowing iTunes vouchers or movie tickets for a job well done.

Of course the omnipresent reward in school is *The Grade*. I believe grades serve two main purposes at school: to recognise the level of ability of a child, and to predict the future level of ability of a child.

Grades can be used to sort or categorise children into classes based on academic performance, and many schools are intent on categorising our children as soon as possible. From an organisational point of view this makes sense; it helps schools determine how many art and music teachers are required as opposed to woodwork or science teachers. But what is convenient for the organisation may not be good for the individual.

The problem with categorising students according to their academic ability is that it is done very early in their development, and there is little upward movement. A child who is in Set 4 for mathematics in Year 7 will very likely be in Set 4 for mathematics in Year 10. We see ourselves as acting positively by identifying students' strengths, but at the same time we are inadvertently telling some students what they are not good at.

Kids identify themselves by what they can or can't do, and these beliefs can become ingrained, often before our kids leave primary school. Teacher and author James Nottingham says, 'If you label kids, you limit kids.' I'd add that by labelling kids so early in their development, we actually limit the adults they become.

The problem with leaving it to schools to tell you what you are good at is that even allowing for all their extracurricular offerings, their view is still typically quite narrow when it comes to the vast array of human abilities. This can have long-lasting implications. How many people believe they 'can't draw?' or 'can't sing to save myself?' How many declare to the world that maths isn't their thing? What implications does this have on human potential? On one's desire to better oneself or seek out new challenges?

Lots of schools have a Gifted and Talented program. Indeed many schools *market* their capacity to cater for the academically gifted. But what about those with 'gifts' or 'talents' in areas other than the school curriculum? By limiting our view of gifts or talents to the realm of academia, art or music, many kids leave school thinking they are not good at anything – that they have no gift or talent.

Josh *could* have been one of those kids. I left for Australia a few weeks after my chat with Josh, but before I went I had a talk to the Home Economics and Art teachers about his interests outside of school. I have no idea whether my chats with either the teachers or Josh had a direct impact, but I was delighted when he contacted me though Facebook three years ago and told me he went to college after 'school got better in Years 9 & 10' and, 'Oh yeah, I'm working as a chef now, in one of Manchester's top hotels.'

....

To find out more about Dan's work visit his website (www.danhaesler.com). To find out more about Dan and Ray Francis's program 'Happy Schools', visit their website (www.happyschools.com.au).

FINDING MY OWN WAY
DR HELEN STREET

This chapter may be considered controversial because it challenges a belief so deeply set in our society, it is often considered a fact. And that is the totally false belief that we can motivate kids to learn if we offer them extrinsic rewards. Young people need to learn to find their own way rather than seek our approval.

This chapter is based on the most controversial talk I have given in my twenty years presenting to teachers. Controversial, not because it presents conflicting views to the research (in fact the research is very robust in this area), but because it challenges a belief so deeply held in our society, it is often considered a fact. And that is the belief that we can better motivate kids to learn if we offer them extrinsic rewards. The reality is quite the opposite.

By extrinsic rewards, I mean everything from stickers at kindergarten to pizza at high school – the rewards we hand out to kids when they do something well, something we want them to do. They are not a part of the task or behaviour we are hoping to encourage, but they come because of it. Rewards are a part of daily life for most western kids.

Yet decades of research from psychology, economics and business studies show that rewards do not in fact work to support motivation in any way. Rather, the research tells us very clearly that rewards actually *diminish* motivation – and they do it as quickly as the child's attentions are turned from the task at hand to the rewards they are working to win. As far back as 1976, David Greene and his colleagues showed that if you reward kids for playing with puzzles they will not want to play with those same puzzles when no reward is forthcoming. In contrast, kids not rewarded to play with the puzzles, will continue to engage in playing whenever they can. In 1984, Leanne Birch and her colleagues demonstrated that children are more likely to lose interest in a new food if given a reward for trying it. Since the 1990s research has been increasingly applied to academic settings. Jeff McQuillan and Ann Boggiano each led research projects demonstrating a long-term loss of interest in literacy when rewards are introduced in the school environment.

Now, before you recount too many tales of how you have seen rewards work well and kids of all ages delight in accepting them, I need to clarify that rewards do indeed have an impact. They achieve something, but that something is not about task motivation. Rewards work to create short-term compliance and obedience. We see it in animal training all the time: many a dog has been successfully trained with a food-based reward system. Similarly, kids will leap to do the most mundane of chores if the payout seems great enough. However, what the research tells us is, these children (and for that matter these dogs) are not becoming more invested in the task we want them to embrace. They are simply becoming compliant and invested in the reward. This means that the more we reward, the more focused on rewards our kids become. This is all very well if you want a well-trained pet who will forever be obedient to your beck and call. It is not so great if you hope your kids will one day leave home and make healthy, self-directed choices in life.

Even if we are sometimes grateful for the compliance we garner with rewards, the shift in focus from task to 'desired goodie' results in a loss of interest in the intrinsic benefits of the task. Rewards not only do *not* motivate kids, they actually demotivate them. Once a child becomes focused on the extrinsic benefits of completing a task, they turn their attention from the process of completing the task. This means they lose touch with the associated intrinsic benefits such as feeling engaged in learning, finding meaning and having fun. Intrinsic benefits are only salient if we are focusing on the process of what we are doing. If we lose awareness of intrinsic benefits, we lose motivation.

This is as true of academic tasks (read ten books for a certificate) as it is of desired behaviour (tidy your room and you can watch TV) and social and emotional learning (I'll give you a present if you are kind to your sister). Whatever the task, it becomes less engaging and less desirable when it is rewarded. To illustrate, I was reading a book with my very self-directed six year old daughter soon after she started school. When we finished, we filled in her class reading log, and the fun she had experienced enjoying her progress and the story content was forgotten as she exclaimed in excitement that she would get a certificate when she had read 25 books. Immediately her attention was removed from the process of reading to counting how many more books she needed to read to get her reward. This change in focus has gradually turned her belief about reading from pleasure pursuit to chore.

My daughter, like many other children self-directed to read, didn't need a certificate to enhance her motivation. The reward did nothing other than highlight someone else's approval and diminish her focus on the joy of reading. Still, some kids are not keen to read, or are even totally resistant, yet even in these cases rewards are more harmful than good. When kids are not motivated to have a go at a task, rewards only add to their disengagement. Far better to ensure that opportunities are provided to read, to learn, to participate, than it is to launch in with rewards and risk long-term disengagement. Kids who start reading later than is the norm, but do so without the temptation of bribery, are far more likely to end up enjoying reading than are even the most literate kids who worked for rewards.

In contrast, the good news is that intrinsic rewards or benefits lead to task engagement and increased wellbeing. Intrinsic rewards arise in doing the task (rather than simply getting it done); they are intrinsic to the task itself. They include challenge, meaning and relevance, increased mastery and a sense of having fun. Intrinsic rewards increase motivation: the more we become aware of the benefits of what we do, the more we want to do those things. Consider reading this book. I would guess you are not reading this because someone is offering you a sticker, a pizza or a trip to the movies. Rather, I am guessing you are reading this chapter because you are interested in the contents.

So how do we ensure that young people experience the intrinsic benefits of learning and living?

The answer lies in understanding our role as a *supporter* of our kids' development, rather than a *controller* of it. We can support young people by helping them to identify the intrinsic benefits in what they do, and helping them to develop an awareness of the process of learning, rather than the benefits of garnering approval.

As both parent and educator, I have occasionally resorted to bribery in an attempt to garner compliance. As such, I know that despite sound research support, the idea of letting go of rewards can leave a very large hole in any classroom management policy or parenting plan. Encouraging positive behaviour and a love of learning is, at least initially, a more challenging process than the instant compliance obtained from a desirable reward. But it is a process that pays dividends in the long term. Here are three strategies that may help you support ongoing motivation and a love of lifelong learning.

Relationship, relationship, relationship

Build positive relationships with children by managing your own stress effectively (adult wellbeing is the foundation of both effective parenting and effective teaching). And, just as importantly, take an active interest in the feelings and aspirations of the children in your care. Ask, 'How are you?' 'How was your day?' By helping kids to feel connected to you and to their world, you are helping them to feel a sense of belonging, which is paramount to wellbeing and the ability to engage in learning.

Self reflection

Ask kids to reflect on the strengths in their own performance before you give them your feedback. Ask them what they have done well, what they have enjoyed about a task, what they have learnt. In modern society we tend to get so caught up with extrinsic feedback, we lose sight of the importance of self reflection. If your four year old shows you a picture they have just created, rather than simply stating how fabulous it is, ask them first what *they* like about it. Far better that a child learns to love their creativity than that they learn to love your judgement.

Seeing the details

Avoid offering the easiest reward of all – blanket praise. Rather than stating 'well done' in response to every vaguely positive behaviour, try simply describing what has occurred: 'I see you've tidied up your room.' Show your interest in a kid's progress by noticing something specific they have done. In this way you will also help them become more aware of their intrinsic rewards. For example it is far more constructive for a teacher to say, 'I see you have organised your report into a clear sequence of steps,' rather than offering the ambiguous: 'Great work.'

Extrinsic reward systems are so entrenched in western schools and homes it may seem inconceivable not to use them. However, it is time we approached them with a healthy scepticism and remind ourselves that compliance and motivation are not the same thing. Young people need to learn, not in order to gain our approval, but to find their own way to be better than OK.

Birch, L. et al. (1984). 'Eating as the means activity in a contingency: effects on young children's food preference'. *Child Development, 55*, pp. 431–9.

Boggiano, A.K. et al. (1991). 'Mastery motivation in boys and girls: the role of intrinsic versus extrinsic motivation'. *Sex Roles, 25*, pp. 511–20.

Boggiano, A.K. et al. (1992). 'Helplessness deficits in students: the role of motivational orientation'. *Motivation and Emotion, 16*, pp. 271–96.

Greene, D. & Lepper, M. (1974). 'Effects of extrinsic rewards on children's subsequent intrinsic interest'. *Child Development, 45*, pp. 1141–5.

McQuillan, J. (1997). 'The effects of incentives on reading'. *Reading Research and Instruction, 36*, pp. 111–25.

STUDENT MOTIVATION AND ENGAGEMENT: STRATEGIES FOR PARENTS AND EDUCATORS
PROFESSOR ANDREW J. MARTIN

Motivation and engagement refer to a student's inclination, energy and drive to achieve and the thoughts and behaviours that reflect this. Motivation and engagement can lead to better results in schoolwork and make the journey through school a happier, more satisfying and fulfilling one.

Student motivation can be defined as a young person's inclination, energy, thought and drive to learn, work effectively and achieve at school. Engagement is the *behaviour* that reflects this. Motivation and engagement refer to what happens in a student's head (e.g. what students think, believe, expect and assume about school, schoolwork, teachers and themselves) and what a student does (e.g. a student's effort and persistence).

I developed the Motivation and Engagement Wheel (see next page) to represent key elements of motivation and engagement, arranged into three groups: boosters, mufflers and guzzlers. Boosters ('the good') reflect enhanced motivation and engagement. Mufflers ('the bad') reflect impeded or constrained motivation and engagement. Guzzlers ('the ugly') reflect reduced motivation and engagement. A Motivation and Engagement Scale (MES) has also been developed for counsellors and other health professionals to assess a student on each part of the Wheel (the Wheel and the MES are available from www.lifelongachievement.com).

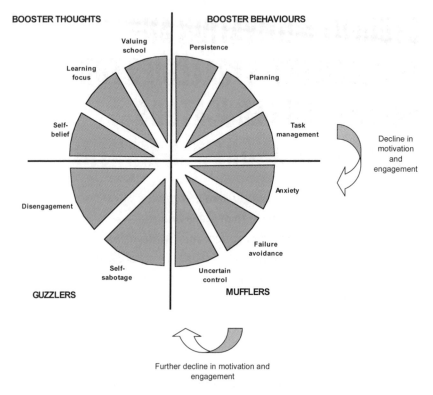

The Motivation and Engagement Wheel
(Reproduced with permission from Lifelong Achievement Group)

Motivation and engagement can be learnt and improved. Enhanced, they can lead to better results in schoolwork and make the journey through school a happier, more satisfying and fulfilling one. Here, I describe the key elements of the Motivation and Engagement Wheel, along with some straightforward strategies you can use to boost and maintain motivation and engagement in your students and children.

Self-belief

Self-belief is a child's belief and confidence in their ability to understand or do well in schoolwork, to meet challenges they face, and to perform to the best of their ability. There are two practical ways to increase a child's self-belief.

One way is to 'chunk' important tasks: breaking schoolwork tasks into manageable pieces and seeing the completion of each piece as a success. By doing this, kids automatically build more success into the process. And each success builds more self-belief.

A second way is to expand the child's views about success. Too often success is seen only in terms of being the best, topping the class, beating others. But success at school also involves improvement, skill development, personal progress, mastery, understanding new things, learning new things, problem solving and personal bests. When you help kids see success in these achievable ways, success becomes more accessible to them. Again, more success leads to greater self-belief.

Valuing school

Valuing school relates to how much students believe that what they learn at school is useful, relevant, meaningful or important. A large part of students' valuing of school stems from their beliefs about school. To develop more positive beliefs about school and school subjects, you might show a child how school and the subjects they learn are relevant to their lives now and further down the track. For instance, school develops their thinking skills, which help in other parts of their life.

Your own beliefs about school are important. You can help foster a valuing of school through showing genuine interest in someone, demonstrating your own valuing of subjects, being quick to respond to problems in schoolwork, and ensuring kids have the books and materials needed to do their schoolwork properly.

Learning focus

Young people are learning focused when they are interested in learning, in developing new skills and improving, in understanding new things, and doing a good job for its own sake and not just for rewards or the marks they will get. You can help boost a young person's learning focus by putting the emphasis on Personal Bests (addressed in detail in my chapter 'Personal Best Goals and Student Growth') and on the importance of the journey as much as the destination.

Learning focused students pay as much or more attention to the journey (the processes involved in an academic task) than the destination (its outcomes or products, such as marks). Processes include effort, learning, participation, persistence, help-seeking and the like. The more you can demonstrate how generally useful these processes are, the more learning focused students are likely to be.

Persistence

Persistence describes how much a young person keeps trying to work out an answer or understand a problem, even if that problem is difficult or challenging. You can help boost persistence by identifying times when the person has persisted before. Here, you encourage them to see that by having persisted before, it is something they can do again. As you discuss these times of persistence, be sure to delve into the thoughts and behaviours in which they engaged. This makes it clearer what thoughts and behaviours they can engage to persist again. You can also boost persistence by means of goal-setting. Personal Best goals represent one useful approach.

Planning and task management

Planning refers to how much students plan assignments, homework and study and how much they keep track of their progress. Task management is about how young people use their study or homework time, organise a study timetable, and choose where they study or do homework. You can assist here by introducing planning and monitoring strategies.

To help young people plan better for short-term tasks, show them how to get it clear in their minds what the task is asking, and spend time thinking out how to do the task, including planning out an answer and preparing a plan for the task before starting it. For medium to longer term tasks, encourage them to think through the steps involved in preparing for the task and construct a timetable for completing it, before turning to the short-term strategies.

Some monitoring and progress checking strategies you might like to share include: re-reading the question after each paragraph is written; re-reading the answer/essay when finished; writing a draft before handing in; double-checking calculations; checking that each part of the question has been answered; and pausing a moment to think rather than writing the first thing that comes to mind.

Anxiety

Anxiety has two parts: feeling nervous and worrying. Feeling nervous is the uneasy or sick feeling kids get when they think about or do their schoolwork, assignments or exams. Worrying is their fear about not doing well. There are some straightforward strategies you can teach all kids to help them tackle their anxiety, though for some particularly anxious kids, professional help may also be required.

The first is to develop some good relaxation strategies: meditation and yoga, breathing techniques, physical activity, sport and exercise. The second is to help them better prepare for tests and exams. This involves identifying what is to be assessed, collecting the relevant study material, and doing practice tests. A third strategy is to encourage the young person to stay in the 'here and now.' Anxiety is often a fearful anticipation of future events. Developing mindfulness and a grounding in the here and now reduces fearful anticipation. Try to help them see that the only moment they can actually deal with is the present moment, so this is the logical moment on which to focus.

Uncertain control

Kids have an uncertain or low sense of control when they are unsure of how to do well or how to avoid doing poorly. One means for developing a sense of control is to develop a *growth mindset*, which I talk about in the chapter 'Personal Best Goals and Student Growth.' Another means is to focus on the things that *are* in the student's control: effort (how hard they try); strategy (the way they try); and attitude (what they think about themselves and about the task). The more you and the students focus on these three things, the more they feel in control, empowered, and 'in the driver's seat.' In contrast, if you, or they, focus on factors beyond their control, such as good and bad luck or easy and difficult test questions, the more they run the risk of feeling helpless.

Failure avoidance and self-sabotage

Young people are failure avoidant when the main reason they do their schoolwork is to avoid doing poorly or being seen to do poorly. Students self-sabotage when they do things that diminish their success at school, like putting off an assignment or wasting time when they are meant to be studying for an exam.

Fear of failure underpins both failure avoidance and self-sabotage. You can help reduce this fear by developing in kids a courageous and constructive view of mistakes. Kids who live in fear of failure are often terrified of making mistakes. Motivated and engaged kids are more able to view mistakes as feedback that can help them improve, and thus have less fear of getting things wrong.

Another way to help reduce fear of failure is to minimise the link between kids' achievement and their worth as a person. This means keeping feedback firmly focused on the task at hand, rather than making overall judgements about the child. Comment on how well the task has been done, not on how capable (or incapable) the student is. The more kids believe that their worth is wrapped up in how they perform at school, the more they fear every essay, test and exam.

Disengagement

Disengagement includes thoughts and feelings of giving up, trying a little less each week, detachment from school and schoolwork, feelings of helplessness, and little or no involvement in class or school activities. To tackle disengagement, a number of strategies are worth considering. Disengaged kids can feel helpless, so the first involves you reminding them what they *do* control – effort, strategy and attitude.

You might also try to determine whether any skill or learning difficulties are impeding their progress. These can include dyslexia, writing difficulties, ADHD, auditory processing problems and the like. If such conditions go unaddressed, disengagement is likely to continue. These students will also require direct and explicit instruction on such things as how to plan and write essays, how to show workings in mathematics, how to research and revise information for tests.

It is also important for you to look out for any mental health issues. Disengaged students can be at risk of depression, anxiety, helplessness and disaffection with the world. Any of these requires immediate professional assistance.

Another strategy is for parents and the school to work closely together. Assisting disengaged students is best addressed through a shared responsibility.

....

Martin, A.J. (2003). *How to motivate your child for school and beyond.* Sydney, Random House/Bantam.

Martin, A.J. (2005). *How to help your child fly through life: The 20 big issues.* Sydney, Random House/Bantam.

Martin, A.J. (2010). *Building classroom success: Eliminating academic fear and failure.* London, Continuum.

Martin, A.J. (2013). *The Motivation and Engagement Scale: A Tool for Assessing Student Motivation and Engagement* (13th edn). Sydney, Lifelong Achievement Group (www.lifelongachievement.com).

Visit www.lifelongachievement.com to find out more about Andrew's work and materials on motivation and engagement.

BUILDING LIFELONG RESILIENCE

ACADEMIC BUOYANCY AND ADAPTABILITY
PROFESSOR ANDREW J. MARTIN

Academic buoyancy is the ability to deal with everyday academic setbacks and challenges. It is relevant to all young people because such setbacks are a reality for all students at some stage.

It is not overly difficult for kids to be motivated and engaged when things are going well for them. It is easy to be enthused, energised and engaged when good marks are rolling in, the work is not too difficult, there are not too many competing demands, and you are getting along well with the teacher. But what about when things are not going so well?

There can be times of adversity in a young person's life, and times of change, uncertainty, transition and novelty, all of which kids have to be able to deal with to effectively navigate school life. The well-rounded young person can bounce back when times are difficult and can adapt when things change.

Academic buoyancy

Academic buoyancy is the ability to deal with low-level everyday academic setbacks and challenges. It is not the same as academic resilience, which relates to substantial, chronic and acute adversity such as learning difficulties, toxic home life, mental/physical health issues and so on. Academic buoyancy is relevant to all young people because everyday and low-level difficulty is a reality for all students at some stage in a school week or term: patches of poor performance and isolated poor grades; threats to self-confidence as a result of negative feedback on their schoolwork; difficult, multi-part or complex schoolwork; competing deadlines; dips in motivation and engagement and minor negative interactions with teachers.

Academic buoyancy is a relatively recent construct and thus far research findings have been significant. Sarah Miller and her colleagues published a paper in 2013 showing that in the UK, academic buoyancy is associated with lower levels of worry, tension and unpleasant physical symptoms during exams. Dave Putwain and colleagues, also in the UK, found much the same in relation to test anxiety. In other research, including my own, academic buoyancy is associated with higher persistence, class participation and educational aspirations. The positive role of academic buoyancy also applies to students with attention deficit hyperactivity disorder (ADHD).

There are strategies you can use to boost kids' academic buoyancy. One strategy focuses on the '5Cs': confidence (self-belief), coordination (planning), commitment (persistence), control and composure (low anxiety). My colleagues and I have found that these factors predict kids' academic buoyancy at school. That is, academically buoyant students tend to be higher in self-belief, planning strategies, persistence and control, and lower in anxiety. You will recognise these factors from the Motivation and Engagement Wheel in my last chapter, which I urge you to revisit for specific advice on how you can assist students in each of these areas.

Other lines of research have associated good teacher–student and parent–child relationships with academic buoyancy. I have identified a number of key elements of good teacher–student relationships, most of which may also be relevant to parents:

- good interpersonal connectedness (getting to know students and being interested in them as individuals)
- the teacher's enjoyment of teaching and working with young people
- striking a balance between authority and a relaxed classroom atmosphere
- striking a balance between serious schoolwork and fun
- the teacher's sense of humour

- making schoolwork interesting and fun where possible and appropriate
- providing students with choices and some responsibility
- explaining work clearly and effectively and aiming for mastery by all students
- broad assessment practices to ensure all students have access to some success
- variety in teaching material and teaching methods.

Adaptability

Through a human lifespan, the world will undergo substantial change on economic, geopolitical, sociocultural, technological, medical and other fronts. Our children's lives are also characterised by frequent change, novelty, variability and uncertainty. They will begin school, adjust to new year groups, tackle new subjects, and probably change schools at some point. In addition, in any given school day, students will change tasks, interact with new people and experience new or changing teachers. Effective kids successfully navigate these changes, uncertainties and transitions. Adaptability, which is the capacity to adjust thinking, behaviour and emotion to successfully navigate uncertainty and novelty, is an important means by which they do so.

Kids adjust their *thinking* to deal with new, changing and uncertain demands by:
- thinking about a new or uncertain situation in a different way (e.g. thinking in terms of the opportunities this new situation might create)
- adjusting assumptions or expectations during times of transition (e.g. not assuming that change is a 'bad' or undesirable thing).

They adjust their *behaviour* to successfully deal with changing and new conditions and situations by:
- seeking out new or more information, help and resources (e.g. asking a teacher to recommend reading

or websites for a new topic)
- taking a different course of action or developing a new schedule (e.g. reorganising their study timetable based on a test announced that day).

And they adjust their positive and negative *emotions* to constructively respond to change and variability by:
- minimising their frustration, disappointment, fear or anger when circumstances change (e.g. not focusing on disappointment when a favourite activity is cancelled)
- drawing on enjoyment, fun and curiosity when circumstances change (e.g. focusing on the stimulating and fun aspects of a new activity)
- managing excitement (e.g. keeping a level head when in a winning position in a task or event).

Recent studies into adaptability are encouraging. We have found adaptability associated with higher buoyancy, conscientiousness, achievement, enjoyment of school and life satisfaction.

Boosting adaptability

There are many ways you can boost kids' adaptability. The examples above are a model for how you can encourage students to make the appropriate modifications when they are faced with change, uncertainty, novelty and transition.

Research has also identified the importance of *control*. Adaptable students not only make adjustments to their thinking, behaviour and emotion in new and uncertain situations, they also take steps to seize control. As I discussed in the previous chapter on motivation and engagement, there are three things in any student's control: *effort* – how hard they work (quantity of effort); *strategy* – the way they work (quality of effort); and *attitude* – what they think of themselves, the task and the teacher. The more you can encourage a young person to focus on these three things, the more in control they will feel. The more you can dissuade them from focusing on good or bad luck, good or bad teaching, and easy or hard test questions, the less they will see their outcomes as being beyond their control.

You can help the student by teaching them how to recognise change and uncertainty in their life and pointing out the benefits of adaptability: making adjustments in their thought, action and emotion. By helping them implement these adjustments, you are helping them deal with ongoing change and novelty.

....

Martin, A.J. (2010). *Building classroom success: Eliminating academic fear and failure.* London, Continuum.

Martin, A.J. (2013). 'The Personal Proficiency Network: Key self-system factors and processes to optimize academic development'. In D.M. McInerney et al. *Theory driving research: New wave perspectives on self-processes and human development.* Charlotte, NC, Information Age Publishing.

Martin, A.J. & Marsh, H.W. (2009). 'Academic resilience and academic buoyancy: Multidimensional and hierarchical conceptual framing of causes, correlates, and cognate constructs'. *Oxford Review of Education, 35,* pp. 353–70.

Martin, A.J., Nejad, H.G., Colmar, S. & Liem, G.A.D. (2013). 'Adaptability: How students' responses to uncertainty and novelty predict their academic and non-academic outcomes'. *Journal of Educational Psychology, 105(3),* pp. 728–46.

Miller, S., Connolly, P. & Maguire, L.K. (2013). 'Wellbeing, academic buoyancy and educational achievement in primary school students'. *International Journal of Educational Research, 62,* pp. 239–48.

Putwain, D.W., Connors, L., Symes, W. & Douglas-Osborn, E. (2012). 'Is academic buoyancy anything more than adaptive coping?'. *Anxiety, Stress and Coping: An International Journal,* 25, pp. 349–358.

Visit www.lifelongachievement.com to find out more about Andrew's work.

RESILIENCE: HELPING CHILDREN AND YOUNG PEOPLE TO 'BOUNCE BACK'
PROFESSOR TONI NOBLE

A key message to communicate to children is that life is a wonderful adventure but one which also has ups and downs. It is normal, at times, to experience setbacks, disappointments and problems.

Katie Walton was surprised when an incident occurred that led to a falling-out with the mother of her daughter's best friend. Katie's daughter Emily, aged seven, had invited her friend Lauren home after school. Katie had allowed Emily and Lauren to walk to a nearby shop to buy an ice-cream. Lauren's mother was horrified that the two girls were allowed to do this and announced she would never allow her daughter to come for a 'play date' again.

Katie had in fact done all the right things to provide the two girls with a good opportunity to practise being independent and responsible. She checked before they left to make sure they understood the road safety rules; she watched them as they put those rules into action when they crossed the cul-de-sac where they live; she rehearsed with them how to make their purchase and receive change; and she reminded them to make sure they stayed together and didn't speak to anyone they didn't know. The girls returned excited by their 'adventure', whose success will give them greater confidence the next time they go shopping.

This incident highlights one of the key issues denying children opportunities to learn resilience. Many children are being over-protected in a way that leads to a lack of confidence and an over-reliance on adults rather than being supported to become more independent, responsible and resilient. Children and young people need opportunities to develop the skills that evolve from being given manageable amounts of risk and responsibility. Risk-taking may sometimes result in setbacks, but appropriate risk-taking also contributes to success and self-confidence.

A key message to communicate to children to help them develop resilience is that life is a wonderful adventure but one which also has ups and downs. It is normal, at times, to experience setbacks, disappointments and problems.

Resilience

Resilience is the capacity to successfully navigate your way through life, to seek and respond to new challenges and experiences and ultimately to thrive. Resilient children are those who are provided with opportunities to develop the necessary skills to enable them to take positive and effective steps to achieve their goals, build relationships, respond adaptively and flexibly to the inevitable challenges of life, and to 'bounce back' from negative events, situations or circumstances.

Young people will always need the personal skills and attitudes to help them bounce back. They will all encounter everyday challenges such as making mistakes, doing poorly on an assignment or test, the loss of a pet, falling out with a friend, moving to a new school or losing in a sports competition. Many will face more significant challenges such as becoming a member of a blended family, the illness or death of a family member, or being bullied. Recent natural disasters such as the Victorian bushfires and the Queensland floods meant that a lot of children faced serious and unpredictable challenges that included the loss of their home, their school and even family or friends.

Some young people face more challenges than others, because they have to live with a learning difficulty or disability or they have a more anxious personality. The more challenges a young person has in their life, the more difficult it can be for them to stay resilient.

The capacity for resilience can vary throughout life, and someone who is resilient in one type of adverse situation may not be as resilient in a different situation or at another time.

Helping young people develop resilience

Resilience is built on the foundation of strong, positive and supportive relationships with parents, teachers, friends and classmates. A child who is connected to what they perceive to be a good school and who is actively involved in their school and/or their community (e.g. through membership of sporting teams or art, drama or dance groups) experiences many opportunities to develop resilience.

Teachers and parents can help develop lifelong skills of resilience in young people by providing opportunities to learn and practise the following skills, attitudes and behaviours in safe and supportive school and family environments:

- *Social skills* – the skills needed to make and keep friends, play and interact with others, have an interesting conversation, successfully negotiate, manage disagreements and cooperate and work well in a team or group.
- *Empathic and pro-social behaviour* – being respectful, kind, fair, honest and cooperative; not mistreating or bullying others; showing care and concern to people who need support; being friendly and not excluding people because of their differences.
- *Self-respect* – this develops from setting high standards for their own behaviour, showing respect to other people, trusting in their own views and ideas (while also listening to and considering others), balancing pride with humility, and believing that they matter and should be treated respectfully by others. When children have self-respect they are also more likely to self-protect and avoid behaviours and situations that present a risk to their safety and wellbeing such as engaging in unsafe practices when using the internet and mobile phones, binge drinking or taking illegal

drugs. With self-respect they are also less vulnerable to being bullied.

- *Optimistic thinking skills* – focusing more on the positives in regard to other people or situations and on things that go well; trying to find the positives (however small) in negative situations; expecting things to mostly work out well and having the confidence to persevere when faced with obstacles; believing that unwelcome situations are temporary (and will probably improve with effort and/or time) and specific (they don't have to flow over into all aspects of your life).
- *Helpful thinking skills* – a type of thinking that's grounded in facts and reality and helps them stay calm so problems can be more readily solved.
- *Using humour in a positive way* – finding something funny in an adverse situation to help keep things in perspective, bond with others and help others feel better.
- *The skills needed to achieve personal goals* – setting specific goals, making plans, being organised and self-disciplined, being prepared to work hard and solve problems; being resourceful.
- *Frustration tolerance* – able to tolerate not getting what they want straight away.
- *Skills for managing strong feelings* – able to deal with anxiety, fear and anger. This includes acting courageously in the face of challenges and difficulties and being able to turn a bad mood into a better one.
- *A sense of personal competence* also contributes to resilience. This can be fostered in young people in a variety of ways. One especially helpful approach is to encourage them to undertake responsibilities such as minding younger siblings, teaching others, being involved in peer support or student leadership at school, volunteering in ways that help others and

undertaking casual employment. Another useful approach is to help them identify their specific strengths (of both character and aptitude) and encourage them to set goals that require them to use and develop those strengths.

Key messages to communicate to help young people become more resilient

- Life is mainly good, but now and then everyone encounters a problem, a difficult or unhappy time or a sad situation. That's a normal part of life.
- 'This too will pass.' Things nearly always get better even though sometimes they may take a bit longer to improve than you would like. Stay hopeful and don't give up too easily in trying to solve the problem. Don't be afraid to ask for help. You will feel better and have more ideas about what you might do if you talk to someone you trust about what's worrying or upsetting you.
- No-one is perfect. We all make mistakes and we all have things we can't do well.
- Take fair responsibility for what you have done or not done that contributed to a difficult or unhappy situation. Don't overly blame yourself or the other person because circumstances, bad luck or something others did may have contributed too.
- If a situation can't be changed, you just have to accept it and live with it. Don't make yourself miserable by exaggerating how bad the situation is or by assuming that the worst possible outcome is the one that will happen.
- When something goes wrong it will usually affect only a part of your life. Try to keep things in perspective by asking yourself: *Does this really matter as much as I think it does? Am I getting upset over very little? On a scale from 1 to 10, how bad is this really?* Concentrate

more on the things in your life that are going well.

- Everyone gets scared or anxious at times but not always about the same things. Facing your fears and having a go at something that makes you nervous (such as public speaking) will help you grow stronger.
- Don't let yourself be 'hijacked' by your feelings so that you are no longer in charge of yourself. Find a way to calm down so you can think of the best way to deal with how you are feeling.
- You can change a bad mood into a good mood if you try. For example you could rethink the problem in a more helpful way; do some form of vigorous exercise; do something kind for someone else; enjoy some good memories by looking through photographs; watch a funny TV show or DVD; read something funny. You could connect with nature – go for a walk in nearby parkland or along the beach, discover what lives in rock pools, or look for interesting living things in your garden.
- Friendships can cause problems. Nobody is born knowing how to be a good friend. Everyone has to learn friendship skills and it takes quite a long time and lots of practice to become good at them. Very few friendships are 'forever' and it is normal to move in and out of friendships as our lives change. Managing a disagreement is often a significant challenge to a friendship. It isn't helpful or accurate to assume that only 'cool' or very popular kids are worth being friends with. Some of these kids are not always 'nice' people because of the way they use their social power to exclude or bully others.

Practical things you can do to help children be more resilient
Don't over-protect your child from the normal challenges that all children have at different ages (e.g. walking to school, looking after their own things, packing their own lunch). Start by giving

your child small age-appropriate challenges that require small responsibilities. Taking small steps moves them towards becoming more independent and competent. Before doing things for them, check first to see whether they are capable of doing it for themselves.

Encourage your child to talk about what's troubling them and help them to find solutions. Encourage them to talk about how they are feeling and what they are thinking about the problem. Then help them to think about possible solutions.

Gently challenge self-defeating talk (e.g. I can't do this, I'm hopeless, dumb, useless) and helpless behaviour (giving up easily, expecting others to do things for them). Suggest they use helpful thinking instead (e.g. I made a mistake but everyone makes mistakes).

Don't fight all your child's battles. Children need to experience some difficult times so they learn how to bounce back.

Avoid offering 'quick fixes' or 'feel good' options when things are tough. Rather than distracting them with a movie or treats, let them sit with the bad feelings, knowing that you care that they are hurting, but that it is something they have to deal with, not escape from.

When something bad happens to your child, help them to keep things in perspective by asking them:

- Does this really matter? Are you getting upset over very little?
- What's the worst thing that can happen? Do you think you can handle that?

Encourage them to think about the parts of their life that are still the same and still good (e.g. they lost a friend but they still have other friends in their team or in the street to play with, their school work is going well, nothing has changed at home). These questions help your child to stop catastrophising and getting upset over things that will get better or improve in time.

Helping children develop good social skills and make and keep friends

Make your child's friends and classmates welcome in your home and get to know them. Discuss beforehand what your child can do to make sure their visitor has a good time (e.g. do things that their friend will enjoy too and not just what they enjoy).

Model good social skills and talk to children about what it means to be a good friend (e.g. be a good listener, have conversations about things you have in common, support your friend when they are feeling sad or worried).

Suggest to your child that all the children they meet regularly at school, sporting activities and clubs are potential friends. Encourage them to develop a diverse social network so that they can interact with and learn about many people, not just people who are similar to them. Discourage the belief that only certain 'cool' or very popular classmates are worth being friends with.

Empathy means understanding the feelings of others and letting them know you understand how they are feeling. Help your child to develop empathy by talking about how others might be feeling and stressing the importance of trying to understand rather than judge.

Teach your child how to negotiate by negotiating with them whenever possible. Look for ways in which they can obtain some of what they want but you also get a lot of what you want – because you are still the boss! If, for example, they do not want to shower at the time that suits you, offer them a 15-minute extension if they agree to get up and do it without any further argument when that time arrives.

If your children are arguing with each other, sit them down and get them to listen to each other's feelings and points of view and insist on their negotiating a solution. Try not to act as referee, but stress that put-downs are unacceptable.

In conclusion

Children and young people who successfully learn the skills and attitudes for coping with life's 'ups and downs' have higher levels of resilience, better quality relationships and a greater sense of confidence. Both teachers and parents can model and teach these skills and attitudes and provide the safe, supportive and respectful school and family environments that foster the development of their lifelong skills of resilience.

Axford, A., Schepens, R. & Blyth, K. (2011). 'Did introducing the Bounce Back programme have an impact on resilience, connectedness and wellbeing of children and teachers in 16 primary schools in Perth and Kinross, Scotland?'. *Educational Psychology in Scotland, 12(1)*, pp. 2–4.

McGrath, H. & Noble, T. (2011). *Bounce Back: A Wellbeing and Resilience Program* (Three books: K–2; Years 3–4; Years 5–8). Melbourne, Pearson Education (www.bounceback. com.au).

Noble, T. & McGrath, H. (2008). 'Positive educational practices framework: A tool for facilitating the work of educational psychologist in promoting pupil wellbeing'. *Journal of Educational and Child Psychology, 25(2)*, pp. 119–34.

Noble, T. & McGrath, H. (2014). 'Promoting Resilience in School Settings'. In G. Fava & C. Bruni (eds). *Increasing Psychological Wellbeing Across Cultures*. NL, Springer.

Noble, T. & McGrath, H. (2013). 'Wellbeing and Resilience in Education'. In I. Boniwell (ed.). *Oxford Handbook of Happiness*. UK, Oxford University Press.

Toni Noble runs BounceBack with Helen McGrath. Find out more about BounceBack and Toni and Helen's many resources at their website (www.bounceback.com.au). Toni is also a key contributor to the 'Safe Schools Hub'. Visit their site (www.safeschoolshub.edu.au) to find out more.

REFUGEE STUDENTS: BUILDING HOPE FOR THE FUTURE
DOROTHY HODDINOTT

Refugees are not voluntary migrants. They have all experienced violence and trauma to some degree. They have all lost nearly everything that connects them to their previous lives. Education gives purpose and meaning to the lives of young refugees who have lost so much. An education can never be taken away.

Year 12 farewells are always a little tearful as students confront the reality of leaving school. Australia's Holroyd High in New South Wales is no exception in this regard, but there is an edge at Holroyd that is not always present in other schools.

That edge comes from the high number of young refugees at the school. Most have arrived in Australia through the humanitarian program or through family reunion; a growing number are asylum seekers. The more fortunate in this last group have protection visas and can get on with their lives; others languish in community detention or on bridging visas, awaiting the outcome of their application for refugee status, an uncertain future the only outcome assured by government policy.

The majority of students in community detention have arrived as unaccompanied minors, either because they are orphaned or because their families are scattered somewhere in the world's vast refugee diaspora: in 2010 the UNHCR estimated that there were 43.7 million displaced people, 27.5 million of them internally and 15.4 million refugees, of whom 837,000 were asylum seekers. Most of these people will never be resettled.

Refugee students have circumstances in common, always violent, which led to their flight. They are all poor, regardless of their families' former social status, education or wealth. They have all suffered loss on a scale unimaginable to most of us: loss of family and friends, home and possessions, language and culture, and, for the majority, life opportunity. Many have suffered abuse.

All young refugees have had substantial interruption to their schooling and some had little or no schooling before arriving in Australia – the average is four years lost schooling. Some have not been able to attend school at all and are illiterate.

Of course, there are kids who are not refugees who also face dislocation, learning a new language, poverty, abuse and so on. The difference is that refugees tend to have more, rather than less of this list, and some have the lot. For refugees are not voluntary migrants. They have all experienced violence and trauma to some degree. They have all lost nearly everything that connects them to their previous lives.

Some have endured the perils of flight, only to find themselves locked up in an Australian detention centre, a daunting circumstance for young people seeking safety and a better life, and all the more as they realise they will be denied any expectation of settlement and the right to an education after turning eighteen. These experiences are not part of a normal childhood.

For young refugees, the opportunity to finish their schooling is crucial, given the challenges of their lives. For them, education literally unlocks the future. More fundamentally, schools are an essential element in normalising the lives of young refugees, in rebuilding trust and hope for the future, and making that future possible. Schools are the best place to address the damage done to young refugees: the healing process starts at the school gate.

A third of all students in Years 7–12 at Holroyd High and almost 50 per cent of students in the school's Intensive English Centre (IEC) are refugees. Overall, about 60 per cent of our students are of recent refugee background.

Because of the urgency of need of these students, the school has to be very clear about what it hopes to achieve and how it can get there.

Our programs are highly targeted and strategic, because there is not much time for our students to make up the gaps in their schooling and learn English to a reasonable standard before they leave us. We have to move our students quickly up the prescribed list of learning objectives and we set the bar high in terms of expectations.

Newly arrived students have only four terms in the IEC to become literate in English, to learn to use technology, and to prepare themselves for the next stage in their education. The pace of learning can be slow, especially for students with low literacy, so we look at what we achieve over the entire period of our students' schooling, rather than at what they can do at the outset. NAPLAN (the national test for literacy and numeracy) provides useful information but as there is no comparative data for over 40 per cent of our students, it is the progression data that tell us how much they have learned.

Our value-added confirms that learning is taking place, at almost double the state average in literacy and more than double in numeracy; nonetheless, we are at the bottom of the league tables. We are also at the lower end of the SES range. The school has that concentration of disadvantage identified in the (2011) Gonski Report.

Gonski made the point that students often experience multiple disadvantage, and that disadvantaged students with a language background other than English (LBOTE), measured by the percentage of LBOTE students and the percentage of parents with education at Year 9 level or below, suffer incremental disadvantage depending on language background, length of time in Australia, English language proficiency, the concentration of other disadvantaged students in their schools, refugee status and visa subclass.

Add prior schooling to the mix. The average length of schooling in the literacy classes in the IEC is less than three years, and what passes for prior schooling for many of our students is not of a first world standard. The level of disadvantage for these students is something like double the average. The most disadvantaged students are refugees with limited English who have been in Australian schools for *more* than a year. This is the point at which recently arrived refugee students with limited English find themselves in mainstream schooling, with varying degrees of support, depending on the school. This transition into mainstream schooling is critical in terms of future success, and particularly important for older refugee students with limited literacy in their own language. These students are at the greatest risk of not completing school.

Schools enrolling refugee students need to be very aware of this and put in place programs to support these students in their transition into mainstream education. We have such a program at Holroyd, as do a number of other metropolitan high schools; however, refugee students in regional and rural schools do not have this degree of support and may have little access either to intensive English programs on arrival or extra support in high school. Subject choices in senior high school may also not meet the needs of these students.

I said before that we have to move our students quickly up the taxonomy. Few children who have been in refugee camps or in immigration detention meet age-related literacy and numeracy benchmarks. Many manifest psychological damage caused by their experiences. The education of refugee children needs to come with a lot of welfare support and provision for counselling, as well as strategic learning programs.

Developing competence in literacy and numeracy is a priority in schools like Holroyd, because without adequate literacy and numeracy skills in English, young people find it hard to engage with further education or obtain employment or integrate themselves successfully into the community. Refugee students need meaningful mainstream credentials in order to access further education.

Part of our success at Holroyd is due to the way we have aligned a rich mix of teaching and learning programs and a wide subject choice, particularly in the senior years; early intervention; and partnerships with universities and business to build engagement and participation and a school culture of high expectations. We have school-wide mentoring and leadership programs.

In March 2008 the Australian government initiated a review of higher education, led by Emeritus Professor Denise Bradley, to examine its future direction, its fitness for purpose in meeting the needs of the Australian community and economy, and the options for ongoing reform. Our practice reflects the Bradley precursors for improving access for disadvantaged students: awareness of higher education, aspiration to participate and attainment to allow participation.

Some of our refugee students have had little formal education before going to university. It takes a great deal of determination, courage and hard work for them to gain university entry and complete their degrees. Over the last five years, an average of forty per cent of students completing the Higher School Certificate at Holroyd have achieved university entry.

Schooling isn't only about what happens in the classroom, of course. A school like ours needs to support students in every aspect of their learning, whether in the classroom or developing a sense of themselves as future citizens. Our code of behaviour is based on respect and responsibility. It is central to everything we do, and deeply embedded into the ethos of the school. It acknowledges and makes explicit rights and responsibilities and assures students of fairness.

Young refugees come from challenging circumstances. Their human rights have been abrogated, which is why they are refugees. When they come to school, they need to see that the school respects their rights. Responsibility is the flip side of rights. Young people who have not known rights need to learn responsibility. Schools play a vital role in this process.

The greatest gift we can give young people is the gift of an education. Education gives purpose and meaning to lives. Importantly, for young refugees who have lost so much, an education can never be taken from you. Education really is their passport to the future.

....

For more information visit the Holroyd High School website (www.holroyd-h.schools.nsw.edu.au).

DEVELOPING POSITIVE
EMOTIONS AND BEHAVIOUR

ENHANCING YOUTH – AND WORLD – HAPPINESS: STEPS FOR TEACHING OUR KIDS TO LIVE HAPPIER LIVES
PROFESSOR GEORGE W. BURNS

If you could have just one wish for your children what would you wish for, over and beyond everything else? The answer is almost universal: 'Above all else, I want them to be happy.'

If you could have just one wish for your child what would you wish for, over and beyond everything else? This is a question I have been privileged to ask many, many parents in the course of my professional life as a clinical psychologist. The answer is almost universal: *Above all else, I want them to be happy.* On a few occasions I have heard: *I want him to be wealthy* or *I want her to have a professional job.* When I enquire further (*Yes, but why do you want him to be wealthy or her to have a professional job?*) the response invariably reflects the underlying objective: *Because, above all else, I want them to be happy.*

Happy people are healthy people. Happy people live longer and enjoy a greater quality of life. They function at a higher level, utilising their personal strengths, skills and abilities to contribute to their own wellbeing as well as that of others and society. They are more likely to be compassionate and, thereby, to contribute to the moral fibre of society in diversely beneficial ways. They are less prone to experience depression and, if they do, tend to manage it better and more quickly. They are less likely to experience anxiety, stress or anger and engage in fewer acts of violence or antisocial behaviour. They enjoy happier and longer-lasting relationships, thus enhancing society's social capital. In all, happy people contribute to society in economic, social, moral, spiritual and psychological terms. Compared to unhappy or depressed people, the happier ones are less of a burden on health services, social welfare agencies, police and justice systems and so are less of a burden on the economy. In other words, helping a child build greater levels of individual happiness during their childhood will not only benefit that particular person but will also lead to the healthy, happy functioning of society as a whole.

Given the worldwide escalation in rates of depression, violence, substance abuse and unhappy relationships, is there any better reason for communities, schools, teachers and parents to be addressing the question: How can we best facilitate the happiness of our children – and, hence, the future happiness of the world? But to address that question, we perhaps first need to ask: What are the factors that contribute to an individual's happiness?

The happiness factors
Fortunately, in the last decade or so, burgeoning research in the field of positive psychology has taught us much about happiness and how to facilitate it. So what have we learned from this research that might be helpful for our kids?

Building positive relationships
First, as a contributor to happiness, positive relationships top the scale. Researchers have explored what factors contribute to the happiness of the top ten per cent of happy people and the answer was clear: the single-most important variable was that 'very happy' people had good, positive social relationships with other people. Relationships are perhaps the most important source of life satisfaction, happiness and emotional wellbeing.

Developing meaning or spirituality
Second on the list of what contributes most to happiness is a sense of

spirituality. Taking a 'big picture' view of life or finding meaning and purpose in life strongly correlates with a life well-lived – regardless of gender, age, religion and nationality. It doesn't seem to matter what you believe in, simply having beliefs, purpose or meaning is likely to ensure higher levels of subjective wellbeing, greater positive emotions and higher satisfaction with life and marriage. Drawing from such information, my colleague Helen Street and I wrote in our book, *Standing without Shoes*, 'numerous researchers have found that those of us with strong spiritual beliefs are happier and better protected against depression than those who have no particular sense of spirituality. Similarly it seems that people cope better with major adversity in their life and major physical illness if they have a sense of established spirituality.'

Finding and using personal strengths
The acknowledgement and use of our strengths is a significant predictor of both psychological and subjective wellbeing, leading to a sense of energy and functioning at optimal levels. Studies with clinically depressed populations have found that helping a person identify and find ways to use their signature strengths led to significant and sustained decreases in depression. The subject of developing strengths is covered in my book, *Happiness, Healing, Enhancement*.

Some steps for enhancing youth – and world – happiness

If society wants to be at peace, happy and functioning at optimal levels, it needs its citizens to be at peace, happy and functioning at optimal levels. For our society to attain those goals we need to start by educating our children in happiness. This means that society, communities, schools and families need to actively adopt policies and practices to foster good relationships, enable young people to find meaning in life, and assist in the identification and use of personal strengths.

In the *relationship* area, these policies and practices need to be directed towards:
- respecting, valuing and encouraging positive, healthy and mutually respectful relationships

- promoting a strong sense of family and community values and ties
- allowing freedom for children to develop healthy, happy relationships
- encouraging the maintenance of positive, healthy relationships.

With regard to the *spiritual* area, parents and teachers could:
- encourage young people to find purpose and meaning in their lives
- grant kids the freedom to follow their individual spiritual paths
- provide freedom to hold personal beliefs without fear of criticism or retribution
- allow them to engage freely in spiritual practices, assuming that those beliefs are beneficial to both individuals and society.

The awareness and use of *personal strengths* leads not only to a healthy, well-functioning individual but also to a healthy, well-functioning society. Kids and teens need the opportunities and guidance to:
- discover their own strengths, qualities and abilities
- receive recognition for and validation of those strengths
- develop and train those strengths
- learn to apply their strengths effectively.

Happy children are more likely to become happy adults. As well as enjoying a more pleasurable and meaningful life, happy adults contribute much to the social fabric of society and its effective functioning and are less of a drain on its resources. It is therefore in the interests of the communities and institutions within society to examine the research on what facilitates happiness and to provide a context in which these factors can flourish. Not only will kids enjoy a healthier, happier and more productive childhood, they are more likely to grow into healthier, happier and more productive adults, thus creating happy communities and a happier world.

....

Burns, G.W. & Street, H. (2003). *Standing Without Shoes: Creating happiness, relieving depression, enhancing life*. Sydney, Prentice Hall.

Burns, G.W. (ed.) (2010). *Happiness, Healing, Enhancement: Your casebook collection for using positive psychotherapy*. Hoboken, NJ, John Wiley & Sons.

To find out more about George, his work and his many published books, visit his website (www.georgeburns.com.au).

TAKING HAPPINESS SERIOUSLY IN SCHOOLS
PROFESSOR TIM SHARP

We need to challenge the tradition of solely and primarily working towards academic goals in order to experience happiness and instead, understand that achievement and success are far more likely to be met if happiness, positivity and engagement are created first.

Teachers and parents – and students – often assume that children will be happy, engaged and well-behaved in school *after* they've achieved some of their academic goals. While this is not an unreasonable assumption, it may not, however, be helpful. Such an approach may well contribute to a phenomenon labelled 'the tyranny of when' and to a range of problems including negative, self-defeating emotions such as frustration, boredom and disengagement.

As an alternative, I propose that rather than waiting for academic success, the skills of happiness and positivity should be taught first. By promoting the 'primacy of positivity,' educators and parents can help children achieve their goals by capitalising on the significant findings of Fredrickson, Lyubomirsky, Cornelius and others and by leveraging off the energy and motivation created.

The primacy of positivity

There is a debate taking place within positive psychology circles questioning the relationship between positive psychology and happiness. Just over a decade ago, Martin Seligman (one of the 'grandfathers' of this field) made it clear that authentic happiness is much more than the experience of positive emotions. Living a good life also involves connectedness, engagement, meaning and purpose. Another leader in this exciting new area, Barbara Fredrickson, decided to leave happiness out of her list of the top ten positive emotions because she considered it too vague a term, its meaning defined so variously by different thinkers.

Some have expressed concerns that the new science of positive psychology will be mistaken for some sort of ambiguous or unhelpfully populist 'happy-ology.' A concern is sometimes raised that the pursuit of positive emotions may lead to selfishness rather than authentic happiness. Findings from social psychology, however, indicate that those who experience positive emotions also have a positive effect on others. This is a process known as social and emotional contagion. That is, when we feel good we're more likely to make others feel good.

As valuable and necessary as these discussions are, it is important not to ignore or underestimate the potentially constructive role that positive emotions can play in a range of contexts, including teaching.

In this chapter I propose that happiness deserves to be taken seriously, and that employing 'the primacy of positivity' is a vital notion for doing so. The primacy of positivity describes the idea that happiness needs to be seen as a precursor to successful learning, not merely as something that arises due to achievement. The primacy of positivity, via happiness and other positive emotions, may enhance the ease with which we achieve success and productivity in our lives. Further, happiness and other positive emotions may also enhance the ease with which teachers can help their students achieve their goals and progress effectively.

Overcoming 'the tyranny of when'

When you ask parents what they want from their children's education, the vast majority will mention things like fulfilment, happiness, love, balance, civility and peace of mind. But when you then ask, 'What do schools teach?' the response is starkly different: things like facts, theories, knowledge, discipline, conformity. In traditional education, happiness is rarely a primary goal; it is more likely a secondary goal or not even an overtly stated goal at all. Regardless, I argue that the appropriate use of happiness and positive emotions is beneficial for all, as almost all students will come up against challenges to the achievement of their goals that I have come to call 'the tyranny of when.'

'I'll be happy when ... I pass this test, when I graduate, when I leave school.' This postponement of happiness until the attainment of imagined and seemingly desirable, but currently unreached, goals is 'the tyranny of when.'

This is not to suggest that goal setting is inherently wrong or bad, or that happiness is the only real goal. In fact Ken Sheldon, a world leader in goal setting and self-determination, argues that appropriate goal setting is one of the strategies that can reliably lead to happiness and satisfaction – achieved through developing goals that match a person's interests and core values.

The problem for many people, however, is that they never get there. If they do reach this satisfaction, often they are soon thinking of something else they 'need' before they can feel happy – the ultimate tyranny, when the goalposts are constantly moved. In recent years, positive psychologists have come to refer to this as the 'hedonic treadmill' in which an individual is constantly running, but never reaching that final, unattainable destination. Happiness is seen as a fleeting emotion that is influenced positively or negatively by events, and individuals never get to experience the level of joy or satisfaction they desire.

This less than ideal notion of happiness parallels popular ideas of success based on the premise that if you work hard you'll achieve your goals, and then you'll be happy. But this is not always true. One important factor is the nature of a person's goals and whether those goals are congruent with their values, purposeful, freely chosen and, importantly, uplifting. Goals can be problematic if they include negative and unhelpful expectations or beliefs.

In 2005 Dan Gilbert investigated affective forecasting, which proposes that people's ability to predict how they'll feel and cope in the future is relatively poor. People tend to overestimate, for example, how difficult it will be to achieve a goal and in turn, may be disrupted or easily demoralised and demotivated by the experience of setbacks early in the process. If this overestimation of the difficulty of reaching goals is not addressed, the attempt to make positive change may be thwarted as soon as a challenge or an obstacle to goal success is encountered.

With the aim of helping more teachers, parents and young people find happiness and success, this chapter proposes a new approach to supporting learning, one that can also be extended to life more generally. This approach challenges the tradition of solely and primarily working towards traditional academic goals in order to experience happiness and instead, argues that achievement and success are far more likely to be met if happiness, positivity and engagement form the foundation. Even if happiness is not an explicit goal in itself, it should still be understood as a highly effective means to other desired ends.

Broaden and build theory
Barbara Fredrickson is most famous for her broaden and build theory of positive emotions. Until quite recently, psychology and psychological researchers focused almost exclusively on negative emotions. As a result, much is known about how emotions such as fear or anxiety impact our behaviour and overall mental state: when we experience these emotions we tend to close up and withdraw, and consequently not cope very well. In contrast, Fredrickson's broaden and build theory (1998) evolved out of the investigation of positive emotions and the discovery that these lead to improved performance and more effective coping and resilience, via the broadening of cognitive processes and increased capacity to build on previous experiences.

Support comes from the work of Sonja Lyubomirsky, Laura King and Ed Diener, who in 2005 reviewed a number of studies and concluded that 'happiness is associated with and precedes numerous successful outcomes, as well as behaviours paralleling success. Furthermore, the evidence suggests that positive affect (the hallmark of wellbeing) may be the cause of many of the desirable characteristics, resources and successes correlated with happiness.' The authors of this landmark study were not referring to an educational context, but their conclusions are highly relevant to this discussion as the range and breadth of outcomes associated with positive affect are impressive – good health, positive relationships, innovation and creativity, to name but a few.

These findings of Fredrickson and others (which are by no means exhaustive or comprehensive) indicate that positive emotions help us enjoy the good times, cope with the tough times and persevere to achieve meaningful goals. Positive emotions are not simply a phenomenon we get to enjoy after we have achieved something of significance, they are the means by which we can increase our chances of achieving significant outcomes. Rather than succumbing to 'the tyranny of when' we can employ 'the power of then.' When happiness and positivity are in place first, the chances of achieving desirable goals are significantly enhanced. The wonders of positive emotions can be experienced before, during and after success, rather than (as we often imagined) only after.

Positivity in education

Definitions of the goals of education vary from 'academic excellence' to 'vocational preparedness' and even the more esoteric 'preparing for a meaningful and happy life.' The evidence suggests that the achievement of any of these educational goals will be made much easier if children are helped to experience positive emotions first. These positive experiences actively engage and inspire a child, making learning interesting, rewarding and desirable.

Such positive experiences increase motivation and innovation, which stimulate creativity and problem solving and drive more helpful and constructive behaviours. Research related to Fredrickson's broaden and build theory suggests that positive emotions enhance creativity, innovation and problem solving, as well as improve teamwork, collaboration and relationships.

Education research reinforces this view, and the primacy of positivity in education is nowhere better demonstrated than in the area of positive student–teacher relationships.

We all have our favourite teachers – ones we remember decades after they left our lives, and whose influences help define who we are today. These relationships are almost invariably the most positive ones, based on warmth, trust, empathy and encouragement. In 2011 Robert Macklin edited a book called *My Favourite Teacher*, a collection of stories from more than ninety high-profile Australians, which anecdotally illustrate the power of positivity in education. We intuitively know that the teachers who genuinely cared about us, who were empathetic and warm towards us, are the ones who influenced us most – and for the better.

And those influential teachers did not wait until we were success-ful at school before they showed us their positivity: they were positive first, as they instinctively knew that their students would flourish in a culture of warmth, acceptance and encouragement – an insight that has been repeatedly confirmed. In 2007 Jeffrey Cornelius-White published findings from a large study of student–teacher relationships and concluded that positive relationships were strongly associated with positive student outcomes. When teachers are non-directing, warm, empathic, encouraging and genuine, students' positive emotions towards these teachers soar, and the students do better at school. And again, the teachers' positivity *precedes* the students' improved performance – strongly suggesting that positivity is causative.

There's no escaping the conclusion that enhancing positivity in children enhances their learning. The primacy of positivity in classrooms pays enormous dividends for our students – academically, socially and emotionally. Positivity promotes improved outcomes, which in turn boost students' confidence and self-esteem and embolden the student to attempt and achieve more, creating an ever-upward spiral fuelled by positivity. These findings beg the question – why wait to introduce positivity in the classroom or at home?

Some strategies for enhancing positivity in the early stages of learning

- First and foremost, develop a positive relationship with a child, regardless of their behaviour (past or present).
- Engage children with something – *anything* – that is relevant, interesting, compelling.

- Actively and explicitly focus on positive experiences in the child's life, past and present (see the work on savouring by Fred Bryant).
- Help children identify their strengths and passions. Specifically look for expressions of these strengths in past experiences and discuss how best to use them in future situations. Do they show a love of art or science? Are they especially good at being a leader or at helping others?
- Build positive adult–child relationships by finding common areas of interest or leisure activities.
- Have fun and use humour appropriately (education is far too important to take too seriously).
- Make children feel special and do what you can to make them believe that the process of teaching is and will be a positive one. This is as important at home and in the playground as it is in the classroom.
- Add value to your children and to the educational process by considering and offering anything and everything you can to help them in every aspect of life (well beyond the traditional numeracy and literacy goals).
- Provide accurate, specific and detailed feedback to children about the task they are undertaking, their approach to that task, and their confidence levels and strengths. Avoid providing empty praise about their presumed traits – such as 'you are so smart' or 'you are a natural.'
- Provide plenty of positive reinforcement each time your child achieves something of significance, regardless of the magnitude, or even when positive experiences from the past are recalled or mentioned.
- Cultivate hope and optimism at every opportunity by reminding children of previous successes and achievements and by noting how these experiences can be used to build more positivity in the future.

- Encourage the doing of good deeds for others.
- Provide instruction in evidence-based mindfulness and meditation methods.

As a meta-strategy, the ideas expressed in this chapter about the importance of taking happiness seriously need to be tested scientifically in schools.

....

Find out more about Tim's work and the references he used to write his chapter at his website (www.thehappinessinstitute.com).

THE FABULOUS FIRST FIVE MINUTES
JULIE DAVEY

During my father's journey with cancer, I witnessed the amazing power of attitude and realised that our levels of health, happiness and success are based upon how we respond to what happens more than what actually happens to us. My father didn't survive the disease, but he had three more years of living, as opposed to a predicted two years of dying.

I first began consciously observing people in 1975 when I 'admitted myself' to the School of Nursing at Prince Henry's Hospital in Melbourne. The course taught me much about the anatomy of bodies and brains but it was the behaviour of the people I worked with and for that taught me the most. Here's what I learned along the way.

Many people focus on, and talk about, negative things such as what they *don't* want; what they *don't* like about themselves, and what is going *wrong* in their world. Often they seem to expect things to improve, but when they focus on the problems, all they tend to see are – the problems!

Negative thoughts can become 'heavy on the mind.' They may lower personal energy levels, deplete the immune system, create long-term negative attitudes, close people off from considering new possibilities and lead to the use of food, alcohol and drugs as 'crutches.' If we want to find solutions, it is more logical, and healthier, to think about positive outcomes. What do we *want* to experience instead? What would we *prefer* to see, hear or feel?

In 1902 James Allen wisely observed that, 'A man cannot directly choose his circumstances, but he can choose his thoughts, and so indirectly, yet surely, shape his circumstances.' Eighty years later, I witnessed this firsthand when my father was diagnosed with an aggressive form of non-Hodgkin lymphoma. I was at work when Dad phoned to tell me that he was on his way to hospital. His doctor had said that treatment could extend Dad's life, but not save it. All Dad heard was 'terminal' and his resulting psychological state was helplessness.

Dr Martin Seligman, the father of helplessness theories in the 1960s, found that the more helpless a patient feels, the greater their level of stress. Chronic stress is known to deplete the immune system, and in his 1991 book, *Learned Optimism*, Seligman observed: 'Optimism prevents helplessness and keeps the immune system feistier.'

On hearing my news that day, one of my colleagues, a scientist in our laboratory, mentioned a book called *You Can Conquer Cancer*, which he urged me to get for Dad. Author Ian Gawler survived an aggressive bone cancer and when fully recovered, wrote the book and founded a healing centre to assist others to manage their health by focusing on what they *could* do to help themselves, including practising meditation and positive thinking.

Dad did very well once he felt he had hope. He accepted the chemotherapy, radiation and other medical procedures. He also attended Ian Gawler's meditation group, installed a tank to catch pure drinking water, grew his own organic vegetables and ground organic flour to make special bread and healthy cookies. But the greatest tonic of all was his shift of mind-set. In between chemotherapy treatments, Mum and Dad headed off on mini holidays. They went to Tasmania, Fiji and various destinations close to home, depending on schedules and Dad's condition at the time. This kept him looking, and moving, forward.

During my father's journey with cancer, I witnessed the amazing power of attitude and realised that life is what we make of it. Our levels of health, happiness and success are based more upon how we *respond* to what happens, than what actually happens to us. Moreover, we choose our thoughts and feelings, and those thoughts and feelings affect our bodies. Most importantly, we are far more likely to be successful if we focus on what we *do* want, rather than what we *don't* want.

My father didn't survive the disease, but he had three more years of living, as opposed to the two years of dying that the doctors had predicted. None of us know exactly how long we have on this earth and it's so important to live each day fully and appreciate what we have.

The FabFirst5

As a result of watching my dad deal with his challenges, I chose to focus on the positive and create something worthwhile out of the life lessons I picked up from him in those three years. One resource that evolved from the experience is the FabFirst5 program, created to remind people of all ages to focus forward; to find a positive possibility in any event and switch their focus to avoid dwelling on 'problems.' It is designed to be taught in school and then practised at home, ideally with all family members participating.

Research shows that children create lasting beliefs and habits well before they reach school, so I encourage parents to consider that their child's education starts at conception. Babies and young children are like hungry sponges, soaking up all manner of information from their immediate environment.

The program has an early-morning focus and prompts us to consider what we want to achieve each day. This encourages in us a sense of control and direction, just as taking to sea in a boat with a rudder and compass is more likely to help us reach our destination rather than diving headfirst into the elements, to be tossed about indiscriminately by whatever life throws at us.

It's very simple. Set your alarm clock to wake you up five minutes earlier than usual. Spend those minutes in gratitude for what is good about your life, then focus on what you hope to achieve in the day ahead. To get clear about what you do want, rather than what you don't, address any worries which may be circulating, perhaps relentlessly, in your mind.

It is well documented that one of the most powerful ways to get a worry off your mind is to write it out. Often a worry can be dispelled just by doing this simple exercise. It's as if the mind says, 'Oh good, now I don't have to keep thinking about that, because it's down on paper.' And not only is it releasing and cathartic to set things down on paper; in the process of working through a problem, writing also allows for clarification and objective viewing.

But it's all very well to know about the science of 'positive focus'; it's the practice of it that makes the difference. The more often that children imagine themselves – pretend and practise – being happy, confident and successful, enjoying their life the way they'd like it to be, the more likely they are to create that for themselves.

The FabFirst5 process helps children become familiar with lateral thinking and gives them the ability to consider things in a new light, so they do not have to get automatically upset or catastrophise when things don't go to plan. They learn to 'look for the good.'

We know and appreciate that the curriculum is jam-packed and that some teachers may want to dismiss this process as 'yet another thing to do' in each busy day. Similarly, parents may say, 'I just don't have time,' although (and you may like to consider this) ...

... It only takes five minutes and the effects can last a lifetime!

To find out more about Julie's work, visit her website (www.aforattitude.com.au). You may also be interested to read Martin Seligman's *Learned Optimism* (1991), which she referred to in this chapter.

WELL-BEHAVED VERSUS WELLBEING
STEVE HERON

Generally, educators would agree that a compliant child is easier to teach than a non-compliant one. But compliance doesn't guarantee effective learning, neither does it guarantee a 'well' or 'happy' child. In contrast, wellbeing provides a firm foundation for both positive behaviour and engagement in lifelong learning.

When we are happy, we are always good, but when we are good, we are not always happy.
Oscar Wilde, *The Picture of Dorian Gray*

....

When I was a child my mum often told me to 'be good.' I tried my best, well most of the time. If someone asked me, 'How are you?' I would say, 'Good.' My mum would quickly correct me: 'Well! When someone asks how you are, you should say *well*, not *good*!' I was confused, I thought she told me to be good!

So what is the difference between 'being good' and 'being well'?

I decided to ask some children. By far the most common answer I received was that 'good' is to behave and 'well' is being happy. Ah, there is a difference.

When I asked children what 'being happy' meant they said, 'You know, when everything is going okay.' When I asked what 'to behave' meant, they said things like, 'To be nice and don't be naughty.'

We all want children to behave well, especially in our schools. Responsibility falls on the principal and the school community to create and maintain a safe and positive learning environment as well as develop effective strategies to manage student behaviour. A compliant child is desirable for many parents and teachers, as their behaviour is easier to manage. In addition, many educators would agree that a compliant child is easier to teach.

However there's no guarantee a compliant child will be a good learner, or a 'well' or 'happy' child, and this focus on compliance could be driven by the false notion that well-behaved children learn better. Our schools could be grabbing the wrong end of the stick.

While many schools have proactive programs for social and emotional wellbeing, often the desired outcome is to create 'good' rather than 'well' children, and in the event, we tend to be more reactive than proactive. Policies that tilt towards reactive and punitive approaches overlook the importance of Social and Emotional Learning (SEL).

SEL programs generally come under the 'Managing Student Behaviour' umbrella. It should be the other way around! SEL is often plonked in Health Ed timeslots, which often comes in a poor last in a long list of priorities in the school curriculum. An administrator illustrated the truth of this when she told me I couldn't conduct a SEL program in a morning slot because that time was dedicated to important core subjects, literacy and numeracy. 'The morning is when children's minds are at their learning best!' she said.

Schools are often pushed politically to an infatuation with literacy and numeracy, not the whole child. But it is no good having a child who can read, write and do sums but who can't relate with others. The famous educationalist Maria Montessori understood this.

> One test of the correctness of educational procedure is the happiness of the child ... If education is always to be conceived along the same antiquated lines of a mere transmission of knowledge, there is little to be hoped from it in the bettering of man's future. For what is the use of transmitting knowledge if the individual's total development lags behind?

Numeracy and literacy are very important pillars in our educational system, but are they the most important? Our emphasis on NAPLAN and on being in the top five nations for literacy and numeracy would make it appear so. Do we think these are the most important skills in getting a job? Are we worried that without them our children won't get a good job with high pay?

Behave well, learn well, get paid well. The formula is flawed.

When we ignore social and emotional wellbeing in our education we do so at society's peril, conclude Aleisha Clarke and Margaret Barry from the Health Promotion Research Centre, National University of Ireland:

> *Although some educators argue against implementing this type of holistic programming because it takes valuable time away from core academic material, our findings suggest that SEL programming not only does not detract from academic performance but actually increases students' performance on standardised tests and grades.*

Growing international evidence shows links between social and emotional wellbeing, behaviour and academic achievement. In 2008, J.W. Payton and colleagues undertook a comprehensive assessment of SEL programs in schools. The review looked at 317 studies involving more than 300,000 children aged 5–13 years. The report, found on the Collaborative for Academic, Social and Emotional Learning (CASEL) website, concluded that SEL programs are intimately linked to improving children's academic performance.

Maurice Elias, a leading child psychologist, researcher and expert on SEL from Rutgers University in New Jersey in the US, writes about the dangers inherent when SEL programs are omitted from, or treated only perfunctorily in our schools. In *Promoting Social and Emotional Learning* (1997), he suggests that many of the problems facing American schools are the result of social and emotional malfunction and a gradual loss of social and emotional competencies. Children suffer from this inadequacy and are left with a legacy of negative consequences:

> *Today's educators have a renewed perspective on what common sense always suggested: when schools attend systematically to students' social and emotional skills, the academic achievement of children increases,*

the incidence of problem behaviours decreases, and the quality of the relationships surrounding each child improves. And, students become the productive, responsible, contributing members of society that we all want.

Other research has shown that children who have emotional stress in their lives don't learn well. Children with behavioural problems most often come to school with an array of painful and distressing feelings and often struggle to behave, let alone learn. When a child's behaviour goes awry there is always a reason why.

SEL should not just be restricted to programs, it should filter through all that we do in our schools. It should touch all of our processes and systems that create a positive environment. It should nurture all of the elements for social and emotional wellbeing for all in the school community.

SEL could be the vital ingredient, not to 'make' children behave well, but for helping them to *be* well. Children can be made to behave well by means of two crude methods: fear of punishment or expectation of reward. Neither creates wellbeing. As Albert Einstein observed, 'If people are good only because they fear punishment, and hope for reward, then we are a sorry lot indeed.'

'Well-behaved' does not necessarily contribute to 'wellbeing', but wellbeing can certainly make a world of difference to a child's behaviour and their ability to learn.

....

Elias, M.J., Zins, J.E., Weissberg, K.S., Greenberg, M.T., Haynes, N.M., Kessler, R., Schwab-Stone, M.E. & Shriver, T.P. (1997). *Promoting Social and Emotional Learning: Guidelines for educators.* ASCD.

To find out more about Steve's work in schools with the BUZ programs, his books and his ideas, visit the Build Up Zone online (www.buildupzone.com).

EMBRACING TRUE IDENTITIES

THE TALE OF A GHOST WHO COULDN'T SCARE: USING KIDS' OWN STORIES TO LEARN AND PROBLEM-SOLVE

PROFESSOR GEORGE W. BURNS

Once upon a time there lived a ghost who couldn't scare a fly. He couldn't scare anyone but himself. So one day he had an idea. He was going to Scare School. He had a witch as a teacher.

How do we communicate life's most important lessons to kids and teens? How do we help them learn, discover, problem-solve and lead happy lives? As a clinical psychologist, much of my lifelong professional interest has been not only in the question of what people, young or old, can do to make life better and happier, but in how we as their mentors can most effectively communicate these important messages to the young.

We can tell kids and teens what to do but, as any teacher or parent knows, telling often doesn't work. Better, we can use the show-rather-than-tell method. But while this has advantages, is it not better still if children create their own learning experiences? We have all heard it said that experience is the best teacher. How then might we best help young people create and learn from their own experiences?

Through all human history stories have been used to explore mysteries, communicate discoveries, share experiences and so enable a person to learn through the experiences of others. Stories have reflected life, communicated values and morals, and suggested solutions to challenging problems. They inform us about the facts of life, teach us values to live by, and provide models for the skills that equip us to survive and thrive. And kids love stories. Just watch how they engage, how their imagination is stimulated and their minds come to life when listening to a story. Given this inherent attraction to stories, the question for teachers and parents is, how can we harness this seemingly natural process for the kids in our care and turn it to helping them create their own learning experiences?

Sam, the primary school age son of friends, is the author of the story with which I commenced this chapter. Sam stated his problem up front: There lived a ghost who couldn't scare a fly. Immediately, I was engaged with both the emotion and the problem of the ghost. What child has not felt inadequate, different, alone, estranged or incapable of doing what might be expected of them? What child has not at least felt they had a witch as a teacher? What would the ghost do, I found myself wondering. How would he solve his problem? What would be the outcome? I read on.

> At the end of the day he went home to his father and asked, 'How do you scare someone?'
>
> His father said, 'It's easy, watch me.' And the father scared a girl who was walking by so much that she dropped her book. 'See, it's easy,' said his father.

Sam's story showed us how kids can develop their own empowering strategies for change through a metaphoric story. Having used his father as role model, the ghost now seeks to discover what he could learn from a book. What other sources, I wondered, could he find to help build his skills in the direction he desired?

> The ghost picked up the book that the girl had dropped and read it. It was about how to scare someone.
>
> 'I'll show them,' said the ghost.
>
> 'Roarrr!!!!'

Next, Sam builds himself into the story and has his ghost acquire another important life lesson: not everything we learn or try to practise necessarily works in every situation or for every person and, if it doesn't, maybe there is something important we can learn from that.

Everyone in his grade had run away except for one person – Sam.

'Roarrrr!!!' This was the biggest he could do but Sam wasn't scared.

'Who are you?' said the ghost.

'I'm the greatest, scariest person in school.' So Sam taught the ghost all his moves.

Using a child's own story has several educational advantages.

- Having created the story, it is often easier for the child to identify with its message than is the case with a story that was externally given.
- In creating the story the child will commonly find his or her own solutions.
- If the child fails to resolve the problem, and does not see the means for reaching a satisfactory outcome, then an adult can help guide them towards finding a solution within the context of the child's own story.
- If you are working with groups of children, or in classroom situations, it is possible to ask the group to brainstorm solutions for the story's outcome.

As the ghost built his skills to become as scary as his role model, he discovered a means for dealing with kids who laughed at him. Because he had practised and developed his abilities, he was accepted among the peers he admired.

'You are as scary as me. You and I should have lunch.'

So they went and the sixth graders started laughing at the ghost, but he scared them right away.

After they had finished lunch, Sam told the ghost to come with him to his club. There they saw three monsters

*sitting at the table: Angus, Nick, and Leigh. 'Hi,' they all
said.*

*'Guys, meet our new President I've been telling you
about,' said Sam. 'All Hail!'*

Sam's tale is a lovely example of the core ingredients of a learning
and problem-solving story. It describes the *problem*, it realistically
builds the *resources* or skills with which to find a satisfactory
outcome, and it celebrates the attainment of that outcome. A more
detailed explanation of this process, which I call the PRO (Problem,
Resource, Outcome) approach to developing learning metaphors,
can be found in my books, *101 Healing Stories, 101 Healing Stories for
Kids and Teens,* and *Healing With Stories.*

All kids have the ability to create their own problem-solving or
healing stories. Helping them to do so is not only an effective way
of teaching, it is a fun-filled, potent and privileged way of working
with kids.

'Now you can join the competition,' Nick said.

*'All right, what do I do to get into practice?' asked the
ghost.*

*The day came and they all went to the contest. After
everyone had done their scare, the ghost did his.*

*'And now the moment you've all been waiting for. The
winner is Ghost!'*

Help kids create their own learning and problem-solving stories
Ask your child to tell, write or draw a story that has a character (an
animal, an imaginary figure, a hero, someone about your own age, or
whoever you want) who:
- has a problem or problems
- finds helpful ways to resolve those problems, and
- enjoys the benefits of resolving them.

Kids will commonly find a problem or problems from their own
experience but if they struggle to do so you might offer an example

such as a succinct version of Sam's story. 'I once read a story about a character that was a ghost. This ghost had the problem that he couldn't scare anyone, not even a fly. Trying to find ways to fix it, first he asked someone, then he read a book, and then he started to watch what other ghosts did and copied them. Some things he tried worked, and some didn't. In the end he felt so proud when he could scare off monsters that were terrifying good people.'

A note to Sam: Thank you Sam for your kind generosity in allowing me to reproduce your story.

....

Burns, G.W. (2001). *101 Healing Stories: Using metaphors in therapy.* New York, John Wiley & Sons.

Burns, G.W. (2005). *101 Healing Stories for Kids and Teens.* Hoboken, NJ, John Wiley & Sons.

Burns, G.W. (ed.) (2007). *Healing With Stories: Your casebook collection for using therapeutic metaphors.* Hoboken, NJ, John Wiley & Sons.

To find out more about George and his many published books, visit his website (www.georgeburns.com.au).

NAVIGATING YOUNG PEOPLE'S SEXUAL BEHAVIOURS
HOLLY BRENNAN

Sexuality is a normal part of life. It is never too early to be supporting children in the development of a healthy sexuality. Talking openly, explaining clearly, can help eliminate shame and embarrassment about sex and provide positive support for all young people.

Adults who love, nurture, support and work with children know that at some points you find yourself talking about body parts, about being private, about touching, about kissing and about much, much more ... including topics like pregnancy, pornography and abuse. If you are a parent or a teacher, being an ostrich with your head in the sand is about the only way to stay oblivious to the ongoing sexuality and relationship needs of the children in your life. It'll come as no surprise that being an ostrich is no good for you and it is no good for children either. The world is full of sexual messages and our job is to help children navigate the messages safely and make sense of them in a way that is appropriate to their level of understanding so that they can make healthy, informed choices.

The talk
There is no single formula that models how you can talk about healthy, safe, informed and age-appropriate sexual expression and relationships with children. Most parents understand that talking to children about sexuality and relationships is essential for connecting in real and meaningful ways with them, and to help them grow up safe, secure and with a strong sense of self.

In fact, the research says that most parents just want a bit of help to know they are doing and saying the right thing and responding in ways that help children develop 'normally' (Latrobe University, 2008; Footprints, 2011). The topics parents report as important include talking about feelings, personal safety, prevention of sexual abuse, sexual development, puberty, relationships, sexual identity, safe sex, pregnancy and sexual health. Parents do not want to leave 'the talk' too late, with an overwhelming majority of 98 per cent agreeing that young people need to be provided with information about sexual decision-making before they engage in sexual relationships (Footprints, 2011).

Sexuality and relationships education

Teachers also acknowledge the importance of sexuality and relationships education (SRE) for the benefit of student health and wellbeing (Alldred, David & Smith, 2003), but often hesitate to introduce it in the classroom for fear that parents will oppose open discussion about sexuality and relationships.

Yet the opposite is in fact true. The majority of parents and carers in the Footprints 2011 survey supported teachers providing SRE at school. As one parent of a child in Grade 7 put it:

> I think the kids shouldn't just get it from home. They
> need a general and neutral view. A different approach
> than from parents. Children can maybe ask more
> questions of teachers than their parents ... Teachers with
> a background on the subject might be able to give better
> responses.

Knowing that parents and carers perceive that school SRE programs help them, as parents, to talk about sexuality at home, makes it easier for many teachers to do what they are good at – and get on with teaching SRE as part of their curriculum.

Children who have accurate and clear information about sexuality and relationships are more likely to:
- feel positive about themselves and their bodies
- understand appropriate and inappropriate behaviours
- understand and accept physical and emotional changes

- be able to talk about sexual matters when it is important
- avoid or report sexual exploitation and abuse
- make informed and responsible sexual decisions in life
- enjoy their sexual experiences.

(Brennan & Graham, 2012)

Understanding sexual behaviours of children

Children and young people occasionally exhibit sexual behaviours at home, at a neighbour's house, in the classroom or in the school yard. Knowing how to identify and respond to sexual behaviours in young people helps parents and teachers support the development of healthy sexuality and protect young people from harm or abuse.

Knowing when things are normal is an important part of supporting and protecting children. Sexual behaviours are not just about sex. They include any talk, touch questions, conversations and interests which relate to sexuality and relationships. Most sexual expressions by children are normal, healthy and safe.

Small children may want to look at or touch their own or others' private parts, ask questions about babies, or play games which explore relationships and gender roles. As children grow, it is expected that they will learn boundaries and cultural rules about touch and privacy.

Sexual behaviours which are part of normal and healthy development are:

- spontaneous, curious, light-hearted, easily diverted, enjoyable, mutual and consensual
- appropriate to the child's age and development
- activities or play among equals in terms of age, size and ability levels
- about understanding and gathering information, balanced with curiosity about other parts of life.

(Brennan & Graham, 2012)

Harmful sexual behaviours are less common. Behaviours that may be of concern are those which fall outside of normal in terms of their persistence or frequency; due to inequality of age or size between young people; because they are not usual for the child or because they risk their safety. Sexual behaviours that are problematic may appear forceful, secretive, compulsive, coercive or degrading and may reveal a child to be acting harmfully towards themselves or others, or at risk of harm themselves.

Being able to identify whether a child's sexual behaviour is healthy, a matter for concern, or harmful is part of providing support. There are various ways that a parent or teacher can help a child develop healthy sexual behaviours. Simply providing information and offering emotional support will often be enough to help a child develop confident and healthy ideas and behaviours. Sometimes a behaviour may be a cause for concern and putting a child in touch with a psychologist or a sexual health professional may help.

Helping children and young people be safe from sexual abuse

Children are not responsible for their own safety. It is part of our role as adults to prevent childhood sexual abuse.

> Parents and teachers can reduce the risk of sexual abuse. Teaching about personal safety includes talking with children about feelings, bodies and privacy, assertiveness, understanding relationships, identifying the rules about touch and knowing what to do if the rules are broken.
> (Family Planning Queensland, 2012; Sanderson, 2004)

Giving information can help. Be positive by talking about children's ability to be safe and focus on strategies rather than consequences. Be factual. Children do not need to be frightened. They do need to know that they can come to you for help and to be safe. Keep it brief. Short, regular talks about personal safety are much better than a long one-off talk.

Children who receive positive messages about their sexuality and participate in a personal safety program that is reinforced at home and at school are less likely to experience sexual abuse (Sanderson, 2004). By sharing these positive messages with your children, you help protect them from and make them less vulnerable to sexual abuse.

Your job is to talk with children, at home or in the classroom. You talk to the children and young people in your life about sexuality, sexual expression and relationships, not because of shame, denial or fear, but because talking is positive and proactive. Sexuality is a normal part of life. It is never too early to be talking, explaining and supporting children in the development of a healthy sexuality. Talking openly can help eliminate shame and embarrassment and provide positive support for all children.

The following books and websites provide support to teachers to effectively deliver sexuality and relationships education:

Alldred, P., David, M. & Smith, P. (2003). 'Teachers' views of teaching sex education: pedagogy and models of delivery'. *Journal of Educational Enquiry, 4(1)*, pp. 80–96.

Angelo, F., Pritchard, H. & Stewart, R. (2003). *Secret Girls' Business*. Mont Albert, Victoria.

Angelo, F., Pritchard, H. & Stewart, R. (2006). *Secret Boys' Business*. North Balwyn, Victoria.

Brennan, H. & Graham, J. (2012). *Is this normal? Understanding your child's sexual behaviour.* Family Planning Queensland: Brisbane.

Darvill, W. & Powell, K. (2010). *The Puberty Book*. Sydney, Hachette Australia.

Family Planning Queensland. (2012). *Traffic Lights guide to sexual behaviours.*

Family Planning Queensland. Retrieved from: www.fpq.com.au/publications/fsBrochures/Br_Sexual_Behaviours.php.

Family Planning Queensland online Teacher Resource Centre (TRC) (www.fpqteachers.com.au).

I Stay Safe: Sexual health (www.health.qld.gov.au/istaysafe).

Rowley, Tess. (2007). *Everyone's got a bottom*. (www.fpq.com.au).

The Hormone Factory (www.thehormonefactory.com).

The Line: Supporting respectful relationships (www.theline.gov.au).

HELPING KIDS WITH DISABILITY
DR KATHERINE DIX

A major challenge that often affects families who have a child with a disability is social isolation. When families and schools take effective steps to include children with disabilities and ensure their social and psychological needs are met, they help foster positive mental health and wellbeing.

In Australia, around 90 per cent of school-aged children with a disability attend a mainstream school. However, two-thirds of these children experience difficulties at school, and only some receive additional support. Helping children with disabilities can be challenging for schools and families. This chapter discusses strategies to better meet the needs of children with disability, by understanding that effective support for children's wellbeing involves efforts to meet the social, emotional and learning needs of all children. It considers how disability affects children and their families, why children with disabilities are at a greater risk of mental health difficulties, and how schools can promote mental health and wellbeing in children who have additional needs.

Seeing the whole child, not just the disability
Children with disabilities are sometimes seen as 'different.' The term 'disability' refers to a wide range of conditions that in some way limit a person's ability to manage everyday living. In schools these typically include communication disabilities (autism and Asperger spectrums), global developmental delay and intellectual disabilities, sensory disabilities (hearing and vision difficulties), physical disabilities and speech disabilities. Severe social and

emotional mental health difficulties are also often recognised.

The real challenges faced by children at school as a result of any of these disabilities may lead to exclusion from day-to-day learning, play or peer relationships, and experiences of social isolation. Having a disability places limits on the things that children can do and may restrict them from participating in some activities with their classmates. Living with any type of disability that leads to experiences of isolation and exclusion can contribute to a child's mental health difficulties. That's why it is vital to see the whole child, not just the disability or illness.

In respectful and supportive environments that see the whole child and promote their strengths, children with disabilities can maintain good mental health and wellbeing. All children benefit from a sense of belonging at school and having positive relationships with classmates and teachers, but these positive experiences are particularly important for children with disabilities. With careful planning and well-coordinated efforts between families and schools, children with disabilities can have their needs met and be supported so that they can participate and thrive at school.

Maximising their opportunities for success is also important. By providing support and solutions that reduce restrictions on their participation, children with disabilities can achieve more. This approach helps to build self-confidence and motivation for trying new things; it also promotes ways of valuing and including all children.

Supporting families

A family who cares for a child with a disability is faced with many challenges that can affect the whole family or particular individuals within it. One major challenge is social isolation. Friends and extended family may find it difficult to understand and support the family's circumstances. Going on holidays or catching up with friends may be distant memories as the family strives to meet the child's additional needs. For these families, the challenges often include the involved process of working out how to access the right services for their child, not to mention dealing with the rollercoaster ride of emotions that can accompany parenting a child with a disability. There may be any number of challenges associated with physically and medically caring for a child's additional needs on a day-to-day basis. These may include managing the problematic behaviours that some children with disabilities have, coping with the need to administer daily treatments, or making sure that facilities can accommodate the child's needs outside the home, such as wheelchair access. It takes patience to help children with bathing, dressing and eating, and fortitude to advocate for the child's needs.

Siblings of a child with disabilities may need additional support. They may feel a range of emotions, such as jealousy because of less parental attention, guilt for complaining about the additional strains put on the family, or happiness when their brother or sister achieves something new. At school, siblings of a child with disabilities may sometimes get teased. So being in a school that takes a whole-school approach to wellbeing can reduce negative behaviour and benefit both the child with disabilities and their siblings. It is also important that siblings have a break from the family circumstances and spend time with friends. They should also have the opportunity to talk about how they feel and get support from their parents, the school or community support services.

The link between disability and mental health

There is a growing pool of evidence that children with disabilities are significantly more likely to develop mental health problems than children without disabilities. The chance is even higher in children with multiple disabilities. A study I conducted with colleagues in 2010 found that children with no disabilities had a 13 per cent chance of experiencing mental health difficulties; for children with one disability it was a 33 per cent chance, and with multiple disabilities, a 50 per cent chance. Some children with disabilities may find it difficult to form and maintain relationships because their disability limits them from participating in everyday activities with their classmates. They may find it difficult to pick up social cues that allow them to participate cooperatively, like taking turns, or they may find social interaction confronting. Children with physical disabilities may be unable to fully participate in games that other children play. They are also more likely to experience situations that negatively affect mental health, such as rejection and bullying. As a result, children with disabilities may lose confidence in their ability to make friends or to participate in activities that other children their age enjoy. The combination of these sorts of factors can increase the risk of developing low self-esteem, or disorders like depression.

Clearly, the key factors that influence the mental health and wellbeing of children with disabilities, aside from the extent of the child's disabilities, are the support and attitudes of others. When families and schools take effective steps to include children with disabilities and ensure their needs are met, they help foster positive mental health and wellbeing. When the child's individual needs are understood, their strengths built upon, and a supportive and respectful environment is provided, children with disabilities can maximise their learning potential and thrive.

Steps to supporting children with disabilities

Build strengths step by step. Break tasks into small steps to help ensure success and support children's learning. Support children's confidence by emphasising what they can do.

Advocate for children with disabilities. Making sure that others understand the need to include and value all children benefits the individual child and promotes a caring community.

Focus on the whole child and their individual needs. Children's needs should be assessed individually and regularly. Avoid assuming that all children with a particular disability have the same problems and needs. An individual child's needs may also change over time.

Build a positive community. Be mindful that children with disabilities have a greater chance of developing mental health problems and act to reduce negative experiences. All children will benefit.

Build partnerships: Parents and carers cannot meet the complex needs of children with disabilities or chronic illness alone. Collaborative involvement between families, schools and health professionals helps to ensure the best outcomes for children's development and mental health. It takes a village to raise a child.

Using KidsMatter to help kids with disabilities

Recognising the need for schools to adopt a population health model, the Australian Department of Health and beyondblue funded an initiative called KidsMatter Primary, aimed at improving the mental health and wellbeing of children. The whole-school mental health promotion, prevention and early intervention initiative provides schools with proven methods, tools and support for nurturing happy, balanced kids. Because KidsMatter uses a whole-school approach, it does not focus on specific groups of children, like those with a disability, but acts to destigmatise groups known to be at greatest risk of mental health problems.

> *I think it's demystifying and destigmatising mental health, because I think mental health, it's mental – you know, mental , it's got a bad label ... it was never talked about. Now it's like fitness or a cold. It's OK to talk about it and I really am enjoying being in a school where that is so open.*
>
> (KidsMatter school teacher)

KidsMatter Primary was found to have a positive effect on children with disabilities by strengthening their wellbeing and reducing mental health difficulties. Below are some ways of using the KidsMatter framework to help children with disabilities.

1. *Creating a positive school community for children with disabilities.* Developing a culture of belonging and inclusion at school is especially important for children with disabilities and their families. This involves finding out about the particular needs of children with disabilities, tailoring teaching practices accordingly and collaborating effectively with parents and carers.

Schools can also support belonging and inclusion by promoting values of friendship, cooperation and respect, and by ensuring that the school's policies and practices address instances of bullying or harassment quickly and effectively when they occur.

2. *Social and emotional learning (SEL) for children with disabilities.* When planning a SEL curriculum, teachers of children with disabilities should take into account their particular learning needs. By assessing each child's social and emotional skills individually, a learning plan can be developed to build skills step-by-step. Select appropriate teaching and learning materials. Breaking down complex skills into smaller concrete steps is important for ensuring success. Opportunities for children to practise should be provided for each step. Providing structured peer-to-peer learning activities, in which children learn social skills through direct interaction with one another, is often helpful. Praise or rewards given for effort and achievement of each step helps to consolidate new skills.

3. *Supporting families of children with disabilities.* Having good support is especially important for families of children with disabilities. Schools can provide support by listening to parents and carers, finding out about the particular needs of their children, and collaborating to meet those needs. Schools can assist families by providing relevant information and links to services. By facilitating access to support networks and professional services, schools can help families of children with disabilities get the range of support they require.

4. *Helping children with mental health difficulties.* Getting help early in life can make a significant difference to ensuring that a child's disabilities are appropriately identified, and that professional

help and learning support are provided as soon as possible. This helps to minimise the effects of the disability and provides developmental support. Some disabilities, particularly those involving learning and social difficulties, may only become apparent after children begin school. In these circumstances, schools can provide crucial assistance through facilitating children's referral for specialist assessment and services.

The KidsMatter website (www.kidsmatter.edu.au/primary/resources -your-journey/mental-health-information) provides resources that specifically support children with diverse needs, and includes information under the headings of:

- Additional needs
- Mental health difficulties and early intervention
- Attention deficit hyperactivity disorder (ADHD)
- Anxiety problems
- Depression
- Serious behaviour problems
- Autism Spectrum Disorders.

At the heart of KidsMatter is a model of inclusivity such that all children with diverse needs, including those with mental health difficulties, are given the best possible opportunity to participate and learn as part of a coherent school-wide approach. Schools can increase the protective factors that support children's mental health by providing an inclusive and accepting environment for *all* children. It also helps to have effective working relationships with services, including clear referral pathways, and to work in partnership with parents and health professionals in order to meet the additional needs of children with disabilities. By paying attention to the mental health needs of children with disabilities and identifying mental health concerns, schools can facilitate appropriate support and make a positive difference in children's lives.

Dix, K.L., Shearer, J., Slee, P.T. & Butcher, C. (2010). *KidsMatter for Students with a Disability: Evaluation Report*. Adelaide, Ministerial Advisory Committee: Students with Disabilities.
Dix, K. et al. (2013). *KidsMatter Early Childhood and Children with disabilities*. Adelaide, Ministerial Advisory Committee: Students with Disabilities.

To find out more about KidsMatter visit their website (www.kidsmatter.edu.au). To find out more about Principals Australia Institute (PAI) visit their website (www.pai.edu.au). PAI provides quality professional learning, leadership development and support to principals and school leaders.

SPIRITUALITY IN THE CLASSROOM
REV RICHARD PENGELLEY

*For too long, modern western education has been
concerned with preparing students for the workplace
and not the world. The universal gifts of story, stillness,
silence and meditation are essential to the development
of the whole person.*

The Industrial Revolution and Enlightenment brought a change of philosophy to the classrooms of the western world. The emphasis on the broad fields of classics, theology, ethics, mathematics, the sciences and oratory began to be replaced by narrower and more applicable subjects such as economics, physics, chemistry, biology, calculus, geometry and the manual arts. Education became increasingly concerned with producing workers and citizens. As the place and practice of religion declined so too did a clearly articulated sense of one's place in the universe and of the good and 'godly' way to live.

One response in Australia was the emergence of faith-based schools in the nineteenth century. Originally highly subsidised by religious institutions, private benefactors and the state, by the mid twentieth century the 'user pays' model had allowed a flourishing of such schools with a wide range of fees and resources. This led to a clear differentiation between the religious and spiritual offerings of state and private schools. In spite of the fact that the number of state school chaplains has increased dramatically in the past decade, this chapter acknowledges the different environments in which the discussion of spirituality in the classroom needs to take place.

A holistic education

The twentieth century also brought the development of a more clearly articulated notion of a 'holistic' education which sought to integrate the layers of meaning and experience to which each individual is exposed.

Holistic education is based on the idea that each person finds meaning and purpose through their connections to the natural world, the communities with whom they interact and spiritual values such as compassion, truth, love, justice and peace. Holistic education encourages a sense of reverence for life and a passion for learning. This may be achieved by direct engagement with the environment, or with rituals and stories designed to nurture a sense of connection and wonder.

It is particularly important when educating holistically to respond to the diverse learning styles and particular needs of each child. At the heart of such an approach lies collaboration rather than competition, and validated experiences rather than achievement. The gentle analysis of real-life moments, awareness of current events and community issues, multiple uses of the arts, meaningful rituals, storytelling, and quiet times for reflection and integration are important parts of holistic education. The need for 'soul room' and 'soul space' are important, the soul being that part of a person that affords meaning, purpose, direction and connection.

Spirituality has an important part to play in such an educational paradigm. In modern western, secular democracies this has often been overlooked. In some ways education has been reduced to the transfer of information as a commodity to be traded for the best opportunities for material success later in life.

All spiritual traditions argue that humanity needs to be careful not to mistake our intellectual concepts of reality for that which is transcendent. Spirituality offers practices and attitudes that can suspend imagined realities so that we might have the chance to notice the wonder and awe that lies beyond our conceptual grasp. This can help to instil a reverence for life as well as capacities to help manage the stresses and strains of being human.

Spirituality in the classroom

Schools with a religious foundation will usually offer some form of religious studies and times of prayer and worship. Traditionally, religious studies have consisted mainly of factual, historical, ethical, denominational and doctrinal information. In recent times, however, there has been a recognition of the value of affective and mindfulness instruction and experience. These spiritual practices and experiences are ancient and time-honoured, and they are applicable to both private and government schools.

Lower primary

At lower primary level, there are many picture book stories available that deal with some of the big issues about life, love, loss and death. If these are read in a spirit of open questioning and discussion with time to sit quietly to absorb meaning before creatively responding, some remarkable responses can emerge. One important skill to teach children is how to sit or lie still with eyes closed and an awareness of their breathing as they allow all of their senses to engage. Out of such centred-ness deeper responses come. Soft music, often gentle classical pieces, can be very helpful to still and relax the children.

Connection with nature comes naturally to small children. Their ability to anthropomorphise animals helps them to see the world through the eyes of wonder. It is no accident that all the great spiritual teachers reminded their disciples to 'be as little children' in order to be open to mystery. Time must be allowed for this, where fact gathering gives way to creative expression about the connections the children see.

Upper primary

In upper primary, story, stillness and silence remain vital. Periods of reflection can go for longer and the notion of mindfulness – a deep awareness of the world around them – can be introduced and named as a practice. At this stage the children are becoming more concerned about what their peers think about them and their opinions. Ethical reflection as part of the discussion about stories becomes more important as long as 'easy answers' are not packaged up for them.

It is also at this stage that children need to be taught where some of society's (and the school's) core values come from. They need to begin to ponder the various consequences for poor ethical choices and why values such as compassion, honesty, justice, mercy and tolerance are important. Ideally, schools and teachers work in partnership with parents to affirm what they have instilled in their children, but this is not always the case.

High school

In middle school or lower high school, stories about relationships are very important – relationships with parents, siblings, peers, other adults, people the students feel judge them, people they may be judging, perhaps a god or gods, and above all their relationship with themselves. Powerful narratives, YouTube and video excerpts and interviews can be very effective (as long as screen watching is minimised – it can lead to 'brain fade' and lack of attention). Stories that touch the emotions make a strong connection with the soul and help adolescents begin to make meaning of their own stories.

Quiet times and safe, quiet places are really helpful at this age. Life can often seem tough, confronting, confusing and painful. Schools that invest in gardens, water features and warm, inviting internal places with beanbags, music, available staff and even a place to make a hot drink can see very real benefits.

By the time students get to the last few years of school, stress levels are rising. The expectations of parents, teachers, peers, society and themselves can see many under enormous pressure. The message 'you will be defined by your exam results' is very hard to counter. In such a rapidly changing world, it is probable that many of the jobs our children will do will be radically different to those existing now, or completely new. As such, it is becoming increasingly difficult for 15 to 17 year olds to know what their tertiary study and career paths might be.

In this challenging reality, the practices of relaxation, meditation and mindfulness can be extremely helpful. If these times of reflection are supplemented with the offer of deep conversations with trusted adults, students may come to their issues with a richer understanding. Again, stories of those who have made meaning of their lives and a wide range of guest speakers who do interesting things out of their commitment to their beliefs and values can be very helpful. It is also important for stories of failure and despair to be told, as long as there is time allowed for reflection and discussion.

Many older adolescents are extremely altruistic and open to positive influence, especially from other young people doing exciting things that make the world a better place. Speakers of all faiths and spiritualities, and those of none, can help to illustrate that there are many different drivers to serving others. Young people of this age are also very aware of global issues and the interconnectedness of all humanity and nature. Many just need direction and affirmation that they can make a difference. If a school is able to provide opportunities for local, national and international service work, that is also a great opportunity to reflect deeply on privilege, poverty, happiness, suffering, meaning and hope.

To conclude

Spirituality has a place in every classroom. The universal gifts of story, stillness, silence and meditation are essential to the development of the whole person. For too long, modern western education has been concerned with preparing students for the workplace and not the world. Through holistic education, individual difference is recognised and honoured and in everyday wonder and connection 'soul' and 'spirit' may be fed. For as Plato reportedly said, 'The purpose of education is to give to the body and to the soul all the beauty and all the perfection of which they are capable.'

Dent, M. (2010). *Nurturing Kids' Hearts and Souls: Building Emotional, Social and Spiritual Competency*. Murwillumbah, NSW, Pennington Publications.

Fowler, J. (1981). *Stages of Faith*. San Francisco, CA, Harper San Francisco.

Leunig, M. (1990). *Common Prayer Collection*. Blackburn, Victoria, Harper Collins Publishers (Australia) Pty Ltd Group.

Palmer, P. (1993). *To Know As We Are Known: Education as a Spiritual Journey*. San Francisco, CA, Harper San Francisco.

For more information visit these websites: www.dialogueaustralasia.org, www.hent.org/spiritual.htm, www.holistic-education.net, www.pathsoflearning.net. Find out more about Christ Church Grammar School by visiting their website (www.ccgs.wa.edu.au).

GROWING GREAT KIDS
PROFESSOR SUE ROFFEY

When we use the term 'great kids' we do not mean grade-A kids, gifted kids, or even good kids! Great kids are defined here as those children and young people who are flourishing in all dimensions of their being and becoming.

This chapter talks about what it means to be a 'great kid', discusses why this is important and explores what children need from home, school and the community to be the best they can be and feel comfortable with who they are. This is what matters, this is what makes a difference to authentic wellbeing, this is what works. But first, we need to unpick some beliefs that are unhelpful in growing great kids.

Myths of wellbeing

Our society is sold several myths, or at least half-truths, about what makes life worthwhile and brings us happiness. Unfortunately these myths are leading to increasing distress in our young people. I address just two of these here.

Passing exams with flying colours. Many students are getting the impression that if they don't get really high scores on tests they are letting themselves down, that everyone will be disappointed in them and doors will be forever closed. No wonder we have high levels of anxiety, in both students and teachers. Anxiety is the most common mental health problem for young people in Australia and it is widely accepted among clinicians and academics that more than half of those diagnosed experience their first onset before they are twelve. Similar figures have been reported in the US and the UK.

Qualifications obviously do make a difference to the range of options available in life, and not getting sufficiently high grades can mean not being able to follow a desired career path. Still, it is important to remember that there are many different ways to reach career goals and a failure to achieve at school does not equate to a lifelong failure. Plenty of students who don't do brilliantly at school still make a success of their lives in meaningful careers which engage their strengths; some of them will later take initiatives in different directions or return to study as mature students.

I once knew two brothers, sons of academics. The younger did exceptionally well at school while the elder had a more practical bent. His teachers constantly expressed surprise that this boy was not as 'bright' as the rest of the family. The 'clever' brother became a special needs teacher and the other a builder, eventually owning his own company. Both did well but you would have thought from the conversations in school at the time that the one who didn't get great results was heading for inevitable disaster. In fact, those who do get excellent exam results might burn out or drop out. Or they may narrow their focus to pleasing those in authority. Employers are now finding that young employees often hesitate to take the initiative in case they make a mistake, and are not very resilient when things do go wrong. Those who have crammed to get high marks may be particularly at risk because they have not learned to think for themselves. Education is more than increasing your knowledge and skills, it is knowing how to use these to good effect. For all these reasons, we need to value the diversity of strengths and interests our young people have.

Stuff and status. We are told by advertisements and magazine articles that having the latest, the best or the most of anything will make us happy. Some parents do not understand when their children are not grateful for all the 'stuff' that comes their way. 'He has everything he could wish for,' said one dad, bewildered that his son was in trouble at school. But the nine year old boy clearly didn't have what he needed most – some quality time with parents who were not at each other's throats.

Although it does not enhance anyone's wellbeing to be in poverty and constantly worried about paying bills, above a certain level, more money does not, on its own, bring sustainable happiness. A lottery winner interviewed nine years after his multimillion windfall was back doing his original job designing and making celebration cakes. He said that no money in the world brought him the same sense of satisfaction. The biographies of the rich and famous are full of stories of being in conflict with the people who are supposed to be closest. Rushing around building up their assets gives them little time to savour what they do have or to just enjoy being alive.

So what does it mean to be a great kid and how do we grow them?

A great kid is curious and eager to learn. I watched a two year old recently in a children's playground playing with a row of chimes. He banged the different pipes in turn and listened intently while the sound surrounded him and then faded away. He then went round the back to see if they made a different noise from a different direction. He was absolutely absorbed in this. His dad was sitting on a bench, reading the Saturday paper. Both child and parent were missing out on some rich conversation that would have enhanced not only their relationship but also the learning opportunities in that situation.

> *I wonder what happens when ...*
> *What else could you ... ?*
> *That sounds like ...*

We hear from teachers that children often come to school with impoverished language. Much of their interaction has been with a screen so they are not used to the two-way dialogue that stimulates thinking. We also know that as children go through school their confidence as learners often diminishes. Children have an innate drive to understand and experiment with the world around them. The more we foster and encourage their curiosity, allowing them to make mistakes and sometimes make a mess, the greater their thirst for learning will be.

A great kid is creative and imaginative. Imagination is an amazing gift. Without this there are no inventions, innovations or problem solving, let alone stories. Imagination enables us to empathise, to put ourselves in the place of others: you need imagination to explore alternatives, play within your own mind and play with others.

You can help develop a child's imagination by encouraging them to 'pretend.' I once spent a whole hour with a four year old playing 'on the beach' in my living room, building sandcastles and knocking them down, looking for shells and crabs, paddling in cold water and jumping the waves – with no props at all except our imagination. Store-bought toys leave children with no need to develop imaginative games, and this has implications for their creative and critical thinking.

A great kid is connected and empathic. Feeling that you belong somewhere, that you matter and can contribute, is a basic psychological need and a protective factor against adversity. Authentic connection is based on reciprocity. When you give children opportunities to be part of collective action you are letting them know that what they have to offer is valued. They can then see themselves as part of that community, whether it is a family, a classroom, sports club or place of worship.

These days there are many children who have a sense of entitlement about their rights but little in the way of responsibility towards others. When parents and teachers have high expectations of what young people can do to support others this promotes a greater sense of connection. Connected kids learn the relational values of respect, kindness, honesty and trust. This gives them a great advantage in developing healthy and sustaining relationships in their lives, one of the most significant pillars of authentic happiness.

A great kid is a good team player. Being a team player means being able to understand that the group goal can be more important than individual success. A team cannot win a match if one person hogs the ball all the time. An orchestra requires each instrument to come in at the right time to make music. Team players share in team celebration and join in the sorrow at losing. Many workplaces require team effort, and those children who learn the skills needed to support teammates and recognise the strengths of others are better able to cooperate in group endeavours – and thereby experience the pleasure that is to be had in being part of something worthwhile beyond self-interest.

A great kid is confident about who they are. Young people are often encouraged to conform, to be like everyone else. And yet everyone is different, each one of us is wonderfully unique. To have and to value diversity brings richness to society. To own who you are takes courage and requires an approach in schools and at home that accepts children whatever their ability or background, even if you are not always accepting of their behaviour!

I have asked teachers and students to devise a recipe for a Confidence Cake. Groups decide on the ingredients, how to mix and cook it, and what would be appropriate decoration. Ingredients have included positive experiences, a large cup of kindness, a handful of TLC, three tablespoons of positive feedback, a big dollop of encouragement and someone who believes in you. These are mixed carefully with a sprinkling of smiles and cooked slowly in a warm and supportive place. The cakes have been decorated with pride and laughter and hundred and thousands of good feelings.

Confidence makes the difference between having hope for the future, believing you can do things – and feeling that you are the victim of fate and everything just happens to you. Children are unlikely to be confident if they are spending all their energies trying to fit someone else's expectations of who they should be.

A great kid likes to have adventures and will have a go at things. Every child has a drive towards independence. This is allied with being natural scientists – kids want to experiment. This is most obvious in small children who throw food to see what happens or press buttons on as many devices as they can reach. Busy parents often find it easier to do things for their children than encourage them to do things for themselves. I heard of a twelve year old boy who had no idea what to do with an orange – someone had always peeled it for him. There has been an explosion in 'risk-averse' parenting where families are either afraid *for* their children and therefore protect them from everything that might possibly harm them, or afraid *of* them, seeking to avoid tantrums at all costs. If children don't have the opportunity to test things out for themselves, they will have fewer skills to make good decisions about risk taking when they are older.

A great kid is resilient and persistent. Some children are never given the opportunity to feel bad, sad or a failure, so never have to learn how to deal with these difficult feelings. When something goes wrong, as it inevitably will, they have nothing to draw on and often go to pieces. Resilience means not being so affected by an adverse event that it overwhelms everything else. Without resilience you are unlikely to have another shot at something – you give up; it's all too painful. In order to be resilient, children need to get things into perspective and not sweat the small stuff. It helps to have a sense of thankfulness for what they *do* have, rather than bemoan what they don't. The conversations around children make a big difference here. How adults talk about events and other people, about what is important and how they get over disappointments, is what children hear and what children learn.

A great kid likes themselves, but also sees themselves developing into a better person. There are plenty of children who are precious to their parents and are constantly told how wonderful they are. However well meant, this can lead to shallow self-esteem, which is not associated with character, effort or achievement. You can only genuinely like yourself if you can acknowledge that you have or are 'a work in progress,' continually developing. A great kid may be good at some things, but is also continually learning, growing and becoming the person that they choose to be. Some youngsters only hear what a nuisance they are or how naughty, and therefore have nothing positive to live up to. Using strengths-based language and helping kids become the people they want to be – holding high expectations that are achieved in small steps – will seed a child who is likely to grow into their own person: complete, confident, self-assured, empathic, connected and able to love life and engage with all it has to offer.

Although this chapter does not give specific references, everything here is based on international research evidence on authentic wellbeing, resilience, positive relationships, optimal parenting styles and positive education.

....

Sue is the editor of *Positive Relationships: Evidence-based practice across the world* (2012), published by Springer. To find out more about Sue, the work she does and her many publications, visit her website (www.sueroffey.com).

PRACTISING POSITIVE

RELATIONSHIPS

POSITIVE CONVERSATIONS
ANDREW FULLER

Communication is a tricky business! Most kids only remember three things from most conversations. If you had your choice, what would be the three things they remembered after talking with you?

At the centre of resilience and wellbeing is our sense of belonging. Belonging is the most powerful antidote to suicide, violence and drug abuse. Our levels of flourishing are linked to the important relationships we have in our lives. The glue that holds those relationships together is love and conversation.

In my forthcoming book, *Tricky Teens*, I describe many young people as the 'New Aloofs' – they are plugged in, digitally connected, but in an electronic bubble beyond which they don't interact, connect or deal with people beyond their close circle of friends. It seems paradoxical that we live in a time when we have never been more connected, yet deep, meaningful and engaged conversations have become rare.

A single conversation can change a life. There is a Zulu saying that people are people because of other people. What connects us to others is love and conversation. Great conversations are like songs sung between people. Conversations harmonise and resonate and deepen our relationships.

The fine art of talking, of getting your message heard and understood as well as converted into some form of action by another human being, is a complicated business. We all have ongoing conversations with ourselves as well as with others, and we can get into all sorts of bother if we assume that the conversations we have with ourselves represent the thoughts of others. It is important to know that what is received is not necessarily what was sent, and that what is sent is not always what was meant.

What makes conversations even murkier is that it often seems that men and women speak entirely different languages. The brains of boys and girls are relatively similar, but the way they use language is poles apart. While there are always exceptions to such generalisations, it is useful to know how most men and most women use language. As we go though these differences it will become clear that the fact that most relationships work at all is nothing short of miraculous.

Men's language and women's language

Men use talk to gain attention and status, to be the chosen one, to assert independence. They often treat conversation like a seesaw – if one person is up, the other must be down. Men are highly attentive to shifts in respect, and the jostling and jockeying in male conversations is designed to answer the question, 'Do you respect me?' Women, on the other hand, are attentive to shifts in nuances and tones, and are well adapted to spot men's lies, brags and exaggerations.

Women more often use conversation to build and maintain relationships. They talk to make bridges between people, and for them, the art of conversation is most often about intimacy and connection. Behind much of their conversation lurk the questions, 'Do you like me?' and 'Am I part of your group?' To build this connection through conversation, many women use talk to highlight similarities. For example, 'Oh yes, I've had that problem too.'

Men and women talk about problems differently. If two women have a similar problem they may well assume they have much in common and could be friends. Men look at problems as things to be minimised or solved. They might share problems and frustrations but will more likely bond over minimising them.

Jokes, stories and pranks are important to boys and men because they allow them to be centre stage and gain attention. It is extremely rare to see a woman at a barbeque call her friends over and start sharing a joke.

From early childhood the differences in language are set. Girls utter two to three times more words than boys. By twenty months of age they have triple the vocabularies of boys. In school, girls play games in which everyone gets a turn. Girls employ turn-taking twenty times more often than boys, and it becomes an established pattern of female conversation. Boys have games in which there are winners and losers. Girls often form close-knit cliques with secret rules. Gossiping becomes a favourite activity and helps them cope with stresses as they feel that they are not alone.

The advice set out below is based on these patterns of language use. Of course, there are many exceptions to these generalisations, but my intention is to cut through some of the barriers to good conversation with information that may not be intuitively understood by either of the sexes.

Advice for women speaking to men and boys
- Ask them for advice and suggestions. Under no circumstance feel obliged to implement anything they suggest.
- Try to see silence as contentment. Boys and men are often quietest when they are happy.
- Talk about activities rather than feelings or 'the relationship.'
- Use data rather than personal anecdotes.
- Know that you will never completely understand the friendly world of rivalry and contest of boys and men.
- Boys communicate in short bursts. Use short, sharp messages. Don't flood them with words or questions.
- Remember that conflict and difference do not always threaten intimacy.
- Understand that watching football is important and is not an opportunity to chat about feelings.

Advice for men speaking to women and girls
- Tame your inner Mr Fix-it! Listen and try to understand before suggesting anything at all. When in doubt don't suggest anything.

- Girls often think, 'If I just get *it* right, I'll get the reaction I want.' For instance, 'If I get such-and-such right, he will love me.' If you can sympathetically support caring behaviours, anxiety can be reduced.
- If a partner stops responding to a woman, she may think he is distancing her or she has done something wrong. If you are feeling unresponsive or needing time alone, explain that you are feeling that way.
- Men don't read sadness in women very well. Ask for details: who, what, where, when and how do you feel about that? Do not try to reassure with a perfunctory 'It will be all right,' or 'Don't worry about it.'
- Details are important. Small gifts are not randomly chosen! Haircuts are for noticing. Kind words and compliments are signs of support and affection.
- Disclose. Share feelings. Use personal examples. If you don't have any, try to imagine what they might be.
- Twenty seconds of hugging increases the feel-good hormone oxytocin in women, which is also part of their bonding mechanism.
- Understand that interdependence does not threaten freedom.
- In arguments don't defend yourself. Listen carefully for as long as it takes, then apologise for your part.

Advice for parents speaking to sons

- Use unadulterated praise; don't qualify (e.g. you did well but you could do better). Don't add ideas or suggestions, just praise.
- Let him know that you love him and respect him. Tell him, then tell him again. Keep telling him.
- Give options or choices wherever possible.
- Boys are more likely to have problems expressing feelings and be more liable to misinterpretations. Be direct. Be firm. Be fair and, if you can, be funny.
- Incorporate a wait time. If you want something done

by 5 pm, start suggesting it about two hours earlier and follow up with hit-and-run reminders.

- Boys are less resilient than girls and may be more romantic. Hurt cuts deep. Don't hover around them using a lot of words but stay nearby and be caring.
- Boys like to score! Competition is fun. It is fine to play competitive games and to celebrate winning, as long as consideration is shown to others and social behaviour remains respectful.
- A flare-up of acne is a clue that androgen levels are high, bringing less empathy and more grumpiness in tow. This may not be a good time for talking about feelings.
- Boys are often most communicative when horizontal; bedtime can be a good time for a chat.

Advice for parents speaking to daughters
- Let her know that you like her and love her.
- Ask her opinion about major family decisions.
- Use direct language if you have an issue that needs to be discussed. Beating around the bush may only increase her anxiety.
- Confide in her when you can.
- If you are having a difference of opinion let her know that you still love her and that together you can solve this.
- If in an argument you need to take a break to let things cool down, let her know that you will continue the conversation later to try to resolve it.
- Let her know that as a family you keep talking about things until you have sorted them out; that you don't let problems fester or ruin relationships.
- Some girls are so tuned in to others that they begin to feel they can read minds. Ask them to outline what they believe you are thinking so that you can add clarification, confirmation or mild correction if needed.

Cultivating high impact conversations with young people

High impact conversations are as much about a meeting of hearts as a meeting of minds. If you think of some of the best conversations you have had with anyone, it is probable they had some of these features: people stopped what they were doing and really listened; curiosity was piqued; jealousy and competition were absent; differences were seen as interesting rather than threatening; people felt able to be authentic and show their vulnerability; hurts may have been talked about but faults were not; and ideas and humour were played with.

The most powerful way to generate constructive conversations with young people is to drop everything and be utterly available to talk – and listen. That does not mean staying around to be abused. Some teens are yet to learn that demeaning and abusing language doesn't work. It is appropriate to say to them, 'I don't have to put up with being spoken to like that. When you are ready to talk positively I'll be happy to talk with you.' Then move away. It is important that you remain true to your values. That is what you are teaching them.

Stay cool and collected. Some teens love drama and will happily intensify interactions. Take your sails out of their wind. If you become aware that you are feeling threatened or agitated, take some time out to settle yourself. If a teen is speaking disrespectfully, quietly whisper to them, 'You're better than this, drop it,' and move on.

Ask mini-questions. How did you do that? What did you do first? By asking open-ended questions that require more than a 'yes' or 'no' answer, you are showing an interest and helping to build conversation.

Don't offer solutions or advice too quickly. If you stick with the conversation long enough, taking turns, they are more likely to provide the solution themselves.

Shaping the outcome. People remember the start and end of things more than they do the middle of things. This means that the way a conversation ends will powerfully influence the message that is taken away. Don't waste this opportunity seeking clarification about what the young person has understood. 'Does what I'm saying sound reasonable to you?' or 'Can you tell me what you got out of our conversation today?' sounds sensible and logical but it frames you as a typical adult. Be the person they weren't expecting, and ask: 'Is there anything else I need to know right now to understand you better?'

Most teens only remember three things from most conversations. If I had my choice the three things they would remember would be:

1. That they are a good person who has the power to change things.
2. That talking to me was helpful.
3. That I am someone who has hope that they can find a way to have a happier life.

....

You can find out more about Andrew's work and his books by visiting his website (www.andrewfuller.com.au).

SHINING A LIGHT ON A BUMPY JOURNEY
MAGGIE DENT

*Our individualistic material world has made it very
difficult for young people to find their true self because
they have so many distractions overloading their mind.
Stable, charismatic adult mentors can help them to
thrive and flourish.*

Adolescence is typically a time of rapid change, confusion and uncertainty, but for young people today the transition to adulthood is even more complex. The modern adolescent lives in a screen-driven world where technology and media permeate every aspect of life, and where young people are saturated with images and information that are often unhealthy and uninformed.

In the Mission Australia Youth Survey 2012, the top three concerns expressed by 15 to 19 year olds were: coping with stress; school and study problems; and body image. These results are unsurprising given the social value attributed to celebrity and consumerism; the massive over-sexualisation of advertising, music, film and TV; easy access to pornography; and the birth of the social media monster, which has seen bullying, predation, peer-pressure, self-harm and narcissism taken to a whole new level.

On top of that, Australia's outcomes-driven, test-focused education system with its competitive nature of ranking and comparing schools based on standardised measures places insidious pressure on students. It says to those who are not academically strong that they don't meet the mark, and to those who are that they must get the best marks possible at all costs.

When you combine these factors with the heightened intensity of emotions that are a normal part of adolescence, it is easy to see why stress is an issue – and why adolescents need a great deal of support.

Providing a positive influence

Never have so many people lived so far from extended family or outside traditional communities where adults served as collective parents for all a neighbourhood's young people. These developments have reduced our social capital – the relationships that bind people together and create a sense of community. We must find ways to deal with our profound loss of social connectedness.
(Father Chris Riley, *Youth off the Streets*)

Young people are highly susceptible to influence, whether positive or negative, and if parents, teachers and other significant adults in their lives do not offer the positives, our youth run the risk of being crushed by the negatives.

Father Chris Riley works daily with adolescents and young adults who are lost. They are not bad, damaged or useless; they are lost. Their bumpy ride to adulthood was a journey without enough loving support and they have been scarred by their choices. I once heard Father Riley interviewed on radio. When asked, 'How can you help these no-hopers?' he replied, 'It's quite easy to help these young people. They all improve with compassion, kindness, food and a safe place to live.' This is exactly what kinship communities offered when adolescents stepped away from their parents in search of independence and autonomy. There were other adults to keep an eye out, guide and support them. These supports can include extended family and others who care enough to be there: teachers, coaches, school nurses, neighbours, a friend's parents. I call them 'lighthouses.'

One of the key things that parents can do during their children's adolescence is to foster potential lighthouse relationships for them, and to be lighthouses themselves for their children's friends. Adolescence is a time of significant brain development and adult allies who are positively involved in a teen's life hold the keys to future success. Even for adolescents who have had childhoods of abuse and deprivation, this is a time of potential to reshape themselves and take advantage of the plasticity of their brains.

The qualities of a lighthouse

A lighthouse represents something strong, reliable and immovable, which shines a light showing safe passage. It does not tell you what to do; it simply shows you a safer way to go. A lighthouse effectively says, 'If you want to do something risky and smash on the rocks below where I stand, I can't rescue you. But I'll keep the light shining so next time you remember how painful that last choice was and you might consider following the safer way that my light illuminates.'

Lighthouses do not rescue; they help young people discover the power of choices, which is what autonomy is all about. A fully functioning adult takes responsibility for their choices, reviews the outcomes and makes a decision. The ability to do this is linked to the growth of the prefrontal cortex, the seat of our executive functioning brain. Increasingly, the 'upstairs brain' governs the mind, rather than the 'downstairs brain.'

A lighthouse is also well informed about adolescent development. It offers friendship and silent guidance, models healthy adulthood, gives hope, and is committed to the greater good of all, not just the pursuit of self. Lighthouses are able to develop relationships with young people in which they can sow seeds of potential and shine a light on the invisible sign that hangs around every adolescent's neck: 'Show me I matter.'

Young people are hard on themselves and adept at self-criticism and self-sabotage, and often get stuck in patterns of limitation. Lighthouses can help them see beyond these limitations and help them find their spark.

Finding the spark for the flame

We need to help our kids find their sparks. We need to listen closely to what genuinely excites our teenagers. It may start with a passion for the electric guitar, tinkering with a car, shooting hoops or another choice that we

might never on our own have thought about as a way to
ignite our child's inner flame.

(Benson, 2008)

In his extensive research, positive youth development pioneer Peter L. Benson from the Search Institute discovered what he believes is the key to helping adolescents find a clearer path and be healthier. Dr Benson argues that every teenager has a spark, something inside that is good, beautiful and useful to the world. It's another way of saying that every child comes with gifts and talents that they need to identify and nurture and use in some way to make the world a better place.

This is why arts programs that include music, drama and multimedia, languages, manual arts and cooking must hold places of real value in our high schools, right alongside the more traditional academic subjects. Better still is the integrated curriculum model that truly engaged schools use, offering students such diverse subjects as surfing, fishing, car maintenance or first aid.

Our individualistic material world has made it very difficult for adolescents to find their true selves because they have so many distractions overloading their mind. Stanford University psychologist William Damon believes that one of the prominent trends of our time is a feeling of emptiness among adolescents and young adults. Perhaps Benson's spark, which is attached to our hidden life purpose and only ignites when we connect with it, is the key to finding what is shrouded in that emptiness. You can tell when an adolescent is connected to their spark because they have lots of energy, enthusiasm and feel driven from within to follow wherever that spark takes them.

Essentially we need to focus more on building the social capital in our schools and communities to ensure that every adolescent has a mentor, adult ally or 'lighthouse' to help them navigate the bumpy journey from childhood to adulthood.

....

To find out more about Maggie, her books and the work she does with schools, visit her website (www.maggiedent.com).

LEARNING TO LIVE TOGETHER
PROFESSOR SUE ROFFEY

Relationships are significant at home and school, at work, with friends and within our communities. It takes more than intelligence and good grades to get on well with one another. So how do we learn relationships? How can we help children and young people establish and maintain positive connections with others?

Four pillars of education are named in the UNESCO report *Learning: The Treasure Within*: learning to know, learning to do, learning to be and learning to live together. The first two represent the knowledge and skills that make up the formal curriculum from kindergarten to higher education: universal subjects like literacy and numeracy and specific disciplines such as architecture or quantum physics. This chapter is about the other two pillars of learning.

Learning to be and learning to live together are concerned with the personal and social development that makes all the difference in how well we live our lives. Despite this, a formal education rarely accords them even equal value with the first two pillars. Emotions and relationships are integral to what happens on a daily basis in every home and every school, and they will develop anyway. When this development is thoughtful or planned rather than incidental or in reaction to crisis, children are likely to learn more positive ways of being and interacting.

Learning to be and learning to live together are critical to achieving authentic wellbeing. The former incorporates self-understanding, emotional skills and resilience, which impact on the quality of living together. Relationships are for many the source of our greatest happiness but also potentially the root of our deepest despair. Relationships are significant at home and school, at work, with friends and within our communities. It takes more than intelligence and good grades to get on well with one another.

So how do we 'learn' relationships? How can we help children and young people establish and maintain positive connections with others and develop the skills and approaches that enable them to thrive, as individuals and in their future families and communities? Our social world is subtle and its navigation complex, but the last fifty years have given us a raft of neurological and other evidence to help us better understand what we need for optimal outcomes. This short chapter can only touch on this extensive literature.

Early childhood experiences

Babies are hard-wired for relationships and begin to learn about these as soon as they are born. Their very first experiences of life are critical. Attachment theory shows that the way a parent or carer responds to their baby in these early months sets up expectations about relationships.

It is in these first weeks that children learn whether or not other people are responsive, reliable and caring. When babies' needs are met fairly promptly they begin to understand that they can have some control over their world. A cry brings someone who at least tries to relieve discomfort. When babies begin to smile they are actively connecting with anyone who comes within range. Adults often put a lot of effort into eliciting that highly rewarding smile. Emotional nurturing demonstrated by warm physical connections and active responses not only promotes a sense of security that enables exploration of the world, but also opens up the baby's cognitive pathways to facilitate learning and provide the foundation for healthy relationships throughout life.

When infants and small children are neglected and their needs are not met, this affects the future functioning of their amygdala, the seat of emotional memory in the brain. The amygdala reacts to perceived threat by sending messages to the body to prepare to fight, flee or freeze. When someone has become attuned to the eventuality of, say, rejection or hurt, they may jump to conclusions about a person's intentions before knowing whether the likelihood of rejection or hurt is real. This does not help in establishing trusting relationships.

As young children grow they want to do things for themselves and establish some autonomy. They begin to understand that they are not the only ones in the world and that the needs of others matter. It is the task of parenting to support the development of independence alongside positive connectedness with others. Socialisation is the process of learning the expectations that enable individuals to participate fully in their community. Parents need to teach their children the basic social and cultural values and provide opportunities for them to mix with others, encouraging prosocial behaviours and positive relational values at every opportunity. The conversations parents and carers have with children in the preschool years can provide a framework for the growth of empathy and cooperation.

> That little girl is waiting for the swing, so you can have one more push then it will be her turn. That would be fair.

> I'll buy each of you an ice-cream but I won't have one, so please offer me a little bit of yours so I get a taste.

> Thank you for helping me tidy up – it's more fun doing things together.

It is not, however, just conversations that determine social learning. Children see and hear what is going on around them and will model themselves on what others do, especially those who are most significant to them. The phrase, 'Do as I tell you, not as I do,' simply doesn't work. If children see relationships around them that are warm, considerate, reciprocal and nurturing then this will form their expectations of how relationships are meant to be – and the opposite of course will also be true.

Primary school years
When children start school it may be the first time they have had to manage social interactions without the direct mediation of a protective adult. This can be eye-opening for some as they find that

they have to abide by certain rules and take others into account if they are to have friends and be part of the group. In the real world people are often expected to work in teams and support each other towards a mutual goal. When children learn the requisite relational skills in school they become better team players.

For a long time the social dynamics of a classroom were considered outside a teacher's remit but with increasing evidence that social factors make a difference to the quality (and safety) of the learning environment, as well as to individual resilience, educators have been asking how they might intervene in supportive and appropriate ways. Social and emotional learning (SEL) is now part of the curriculum in many schools, but to be effective and sustainable, it needs to be delivered in an engaged approach that addresses issues in ways that are safe for both teachers and students and embedded in everyday practice.

A safe and effective way to teach SEL is through the use of interactive games focused on relevant issues. This enables discussion to take place that does not involve personal disclosure but facilitates reflection on situations, needs and different ways of thinking. When students are taken out of their usual social networks and assigned to new groups in these games, they learn to interact with everyone. This breaks down stereotypes and promotes a more positive and inclusive classroom.

Here are some other strategies teachers have used to present SEL:

- Introducing relational values overtly by giving students opportunities to talk about concepts like respect, trust, friendship and kindness, to reflect on what they mean and what happens when they are put into practice.
- Valuing diversity and acknowledging individual strengths as well as seeking our shared humanity and what we have in common.
- Giving young people the agency to define the values/guidelines/rules that promote a positive and inclusive classroom where everyone feels good about being there.

- Teaching and encouraging positive communication skills, including a vocabulary for feelings so that children learn to talk through issues rather than use their fists or feet if a conflict arises.
- Setting up a system of 'personal bests' so that children are more focused on their own incremental achievements rather than competing with others.
- Developing cooperative, interdependent learning strategies so students work together and contribute their individual strengths to group projects.

Adolescence

Learning to be and learning to live together continue to be important as children grow, but issues may change. Teenagers look to their friends to help them establish their own identity and values. This transition involves negotiating a number of relationships – within the family; in the groups they belong to; in school; with early romantic or sexual partners and of course the relationship with themselves and who they are becoming. Young people who have had supportive experiences and the opportunity to reflect on relational values and develop interpersonal competencies – including the ability to deal with conflict and difference – are in a stronger position to weather the storms that adolescence inevitably brings.

How relationships are portrayed in the media can influence expectations about what is 'normal' and this is not always what is healthy. There is a dearth of positive messages in many TV shows, and poor relational attitudes and behaviour are too often displayed by public figures. Meanwhile, social media exerts an increasingly powerful force, with positive and negative effects on relationship development. All these can impact on how a young person learns to perceive and treat others. For example, homophobia or racism in the community leads to intolerance or harassment of individuals; pornography that treats women brutally will influence how sexual relationships are perceived; bullying behaviour that is seen as amusing or 'cool' gives the message that this is acceptable. Young people may come to see others as inferior or expendable.

Relationships that are primarily self-serving and focused on power, control and putting others down are rarely healthy or sustainable and do little for the long-term wellbeing of anyone involved.

Young people therefore need regular opportunities to reflect on and explore what a positive relationship is; how various kinds of interaction make people feel about themselves and their world; what helps them feel connected or be resilient; and what they can offer others. The adults in teenagers' lives might be taking a back seat in some respects, but how they model the management of this developmental stage, how they communicate, and what values they demonstrate will continue to be part of the learning process for young people.

People often only address relationship issues when they are in crisis. We owe it to every child – and to the future wellbeing of our communities – to ensure that our young people are learning the things they need in order to establish and maintain positive relationships and a positive sense of self.

To find out more about Sue, her books, and the work she does on behaviour and social and emotional learning, visit her website (www.sueroffey.com).

THE PARENT–TEACHER PARTNERSHIP
DR JOHN IRVINE

Dear Dr John

As a school principal, I can't count the number of times we've tried to find out why a student has a bad attitude to school and we find the parents have bad and bitter memories of their own school days. School let many of us down, sometimes it bullied kids, or it was cruel to them; education was based on fear, not love of learning, and sometimes parents carry those fears and feelings over and through their children. The school of today is much more approachable, it wants to work with families, it recognises that the family is the most important influence in the child's life.

I'd like to think I'm available to parents at any time so that they can discuss issues before they become problems. It is unlikely that the school their child attends resembles the school they attended. I plead with parents: 'Rather than colour your child's experience with your own, go into your child's school, read newsletters from the school, ask questions and find out about your child's school as it is. In this way your children can enjoy the benefit of your experience of their school which hopefully can become your school as well.'

Yours, Brian

Brian's note is a reminder to me that where parents and school don't work together the result can be catastrophic. As with a warring couple, the child has to take sides. And whoever the child sides with, the other is devalued – family or education. Of course, times have changed. It's not so easy to get up and help out at reading group or go to P&C or P&F meetings. The many mothers who return to the workforce while their children are still young no longer have the free time to act as parent helper at school, however much many would like to. Fathers work an average 47 hours (equivalent to a six-day week), plus commuting time, and are hardly in the mood to help with homework let alone be actively involved in their children's school life when they get home. This is unfortunate, for as psychologist Steve Biddulph has pointed out in his acclaimed book, *Raising Boys*, children whose fathers are involved in their lives do better in schoolwork, especially maths for some reason, and are less likely to get into trouble at school. We can decry the situation or do something about it. Government departments, for instance, could take a proactive role to make it possible for parents to spend more time in the community – through paid time off or time in lieu, or making community service a condition for promotion. If business wants healthy homes and communities it could offer its own incentives for its workers to spend time back in the community.

In the meantime, for the sake of our kids' success at school and for community cohesion, we have to find or make the time to get behind the school and their extracurricular activities. Let me suggest a few ways in which we can do this.

Parents with expertise in any area (model making, beekeeping, invention, joinery, dressmaking, animal care, dentistry, pottery, yoga, art, ceramics) can share their passion with their child's class.

Parents can assist the teacher in costume making, teacher aid design, equipment donations, sharpening pencils.

Parents can assist the school by taking on lollipop duties at crossings or having a weekend working bee at home to cover library books.

Parents can help by listening to little kids learn to read. Research shows that teachers only manage an average 10 to 30 seconds one-to-one time with individual children per day. Extra hands, hugs, ears and words of encouragement are urgently needed.

Parents can help by coaching a sporting team or being an extra adult on school camps.

Parents can help by just having time to hear about their kids' day and be the ears and shoulders kids need to work their way through school.

The evidence for parent involvement is so strong, I would like school enrolment forms to include a section asking parents not *if*, but *how* they're going to be involved in making sure that parents and teachers are partners in education. Remember, it's not what we say or how much we pay that will make school a success, it's what we do that makes the difference.

Ten commandments to parents for educational salvation
(Adapted from Rimm's Laws by Sylvia Rimm)

1. Parents shall honour one another (where more than one exists) and shall honour the school if they expect their children to honour them.
2. Parents shall model good behaviour if they expect good behaviour from kids, because good behaviour is more caught than taught.
3. Parents shall say good things about their kids to other adults, while in their kids' hearing. (What adults say to each other about kids has a profound effect on kids' behaviour, good and bad, and on their self image.)
4. Parents shall not overreact to children's successes or failures or the kids will come to fear the pressure to succeed and despair in failure.
5. Parents shall remember that self-confidence in kids is developed not through indulgence but through effort, so don't make the path too smooth or they'll slip off it.
6. Parents shall remember that children must crawl before they walk, therefore hand over the reins steadily and gradually over time so they develop confidence and self-control.

7. Parents shall remember that any family that is divided against itself or against the school will have children divided against authority.
8. Parents shall consider how they will deal with the fallout before embarking on any confrontation with their children. If you know a child will be upset, consider how you will deal with that before you begin.
9. Parents shall not protect their child from all forms of competition – while over-competitiveness is a sure way for kids to feel inadequate, competition is itself one important way children learn to achieve.
10. Parents shall prioritise efforts to show how their own and their children's learning connects with living if they want their children to view learning as living.

....

Biddulph, S. (2003). *Raising Boys* (revised edition). Finch, Australia.

Rimm, S. (1996). *Why bright kids get poor grades: And what you can do about it.* Three Rivers Press, New York.

If you want to find out more about John, his books and the work he does, visit Dr John's Happy Families website (www.drjohnshappyfamilies.com.au).

GROWING UP IN

NURTURING ENVIRONMENTS

NATURE-GUIDED THERAPY: USING NATURE TO BUILD HAPPIER AND HEALTHIER KIDS
PROFESSOR GEORGE W. BURNS

Kids and nature fit together like a hand in a glove. Helping young people reach this connection is to help them build positive emotions, learn about mindful engagement, develop positive relationships and find both accomplishment and meaning in their lives.

What kid doesn't usually jump at the opportunity to play in a park, visit the beach or go camping in the bush? Explore the sensory experiences to be had in a forest, feel the texture and temperature of sand under their feet, or play with a friendly animal? Indeed, what adult doesn't want to escape the day-to-day pressures of life in just the same way? Have you ever wondered about why this is so or about how we as parents or teachers of the rising generation might be able to use this to enhance our children's learning, their levels of happiness and physical wellbeing?

Throughout human history, survival has depended upon us developing a 'biological fit' with nature. We have had to adapt to our natural environment for the sake of our physical, psychological, social and spiritual wellbeing. In recent centuries – a very brief time in our evolutionary history – we have gone from nomadic to agrarian to high-density, highly urbanised environments that have wrought an increasing detachment from our historic and evolutionary connections with nature. Growing industrialisation, urbanisation and technological advances have outstripped our biological evolution, resulting in a harmful effect on our personal wellbeing, as seen in escalating rates of depression, individual and community emotional discontent and physical disease in the urbanised, developed world. We live in a vastly different environment from the one in which we evolved.

Getting back to nature is generally more aesthetically pleasing and satisfying. The stimuli of nature tend to fit with our senses better than the stimuli of human-constructed environments. To most people an ocean or river view, or the sight of a towering tree, is more inherently pleasurable than the view of a shopping mall, freeway traffic, or towering box-shaped buildings.

Being in nature is beneficial to us physically, psychologically, socially and spiritually. There is an abundance of research information to support this claim, and if you wish to review that, I refer you to my book, *Nature-Guided Therapy*, the result of some four years study of the literature in this area. In this short chapter I will cut to the chase.

When we are in nature we feel physically better, our bodies function at optimal levels of wellbeing and we tend to engage less in unhealthy habits. When we are in natural places that are safe and comfortable for us, we feel more relaxed, happier and at peace; we tend to relate better socially and have a greater sense of spiritual wellbeing. Who hasn't stood at the base of a powerful waterfall and experienced a sense of awe?

Even our ability to learn is enhanced in conducive natural environments. Children who suffer attention deficit hyperactivity disorder (ADHD) experience an increased focus of attention, are better able to complete tasks and are better at following instructions when they have lessons outdoors in a natural environment rather than inside a classroom.

Nature satisfies our senses at many levels and thus meets many of the core needs that positive psychology shows are important to our happiness. It can provide us with a range of positive emotions and engage and absorb us in experiences such as watching a waterfall or sunset. It can enhance our connectedness with other people and it can offer meaning. At times, we might experience a sense of achievement or accomplishment, depending on what we're doing in nature.

Using nature to build happier and healthier kids

Because it is our senses that bring us into contact with nature, the strategies and interventions of Nature-Guided Therapy focus attention on an awareness and employment of sensory experiences. An awareness of sensory information enables us to connect with our environment in a variety of powerful ways. We are often so distracted by our thoughts, we fail to even see the world around us. Yet feeling connected with our environment is an important facet of feeling connected with life. Consider the power of a familiar smell to trigger a memory, or a powerful vista to inspire emotion.

1. *Heightening sensory awareness through imagery.* Invite children to picture themselves in a place in nature where they feel happy, relaxed and content. If they choose the beach, you can focus the awareness on each of their senses of sight, sound, smell, taste and touch in turn: 'Tell me about the different colours, shapes and movements you see in the waves. What are the different sounds you hear and how do they vary? What different things can you smell? Are there any taste sensations you can notice on your lips, your tongue or in your mouth? What are the things you can feel on your skin, like the temperature or the touch of the breeze?'

2. *Heightening sensory awareness in the field.* When engaged in nature activities with children, you might have them lie on the grass and look at the sky, observing the different shades of blue in the sky or the shapes, colours and movement of the clouds (sight). You can invite them to listen to the volume, rhythm and tone of the breeze in the trees (sound). Or focus attention on the smells, fragrances and aromas in the air (smell). Are there any taste sensations, such as the taste of salt on a sea breeze, a child can be aware

of? Tactile sensations might include the cool of a sea breeze, the warmth of the sun or the firmness, texture or temperature of the ground where they're lying (touch).

3. *Creating nature-based activities.* What are the things that your children enjoy doing? Walking, cycling, swimming, running, playing? To maximise the creation of positive emotions, help a child to build awareness of their surroundings when doing the things they enjoy in natural environments, safe and under adult guidance. These sensations can help them relax, improve mood or shift cognitions. In experientially learning the things that enhance their wellbeing, children are building essentials skills for a happy, well-adjusted adulthood.

4. *Creating nature-based mindfulness.* Research is showing us that mindfulness, meditation and focused thinking are important ingredients in a life well lived. Learning this at an early age is a useful skill for a child or adolescent to acquire. As nature is conducive to mindfulness or focused awareness, the two fit comfortably together. Children can be taught, either in imagery or in practice, to quietly sit for three to four minutes, mindfully attending to each sense modality.

Kids generally love being in and interacting with nature. Nature, in itself, is conducive to our physical, psychological, social and spiritual wellbeing. Kids and nature fit together like a hand in a glove. Facilitating young people to make this connection helps them build positive emotions, learn about mindful engagement, develop positive relationships and find accomplishment and meaning in their lives. At the very least, it is a fun and positive way for kids to learn essential life skills, as well as a positive way for us, as their mentors, to interact with them.

Burns, G.W. (1998). *Nature-Guided Therapy: Brief Integrative Strategies for Health and Wellbeing*. Brunner/Mazel, Philadelphia.

To find out more about George and his many published books, visit his website (www.georgeburns.com.au).

BESIDE THE BLOWHOLE
NATALIE HOUGHTON

World renowned primatologist Dr Jane Goodall knows that to save chimpanzees from extinction, we need to consider the needs of the people who live near their habitats. We need to take a holistic approach. Jane is a champion solutionary.

There, beside the blowhole on a beach in Eden, New South Wales, I realised my twenty years in the pastoral industry represented a complete paradox.

From a young girl innately aware of the sentience of animals, to a woman co-managing sheep and cattle stations and participating in a culture tarnished by a tolerance for violence, my journey had led me here to the side of a whale on a beach in New South Wales. It was ironic for someone who had spent her life in inland Australia to be called to save a whale, but here I was. The sun was rising east of Eden, lighting the sand where I knelt splashing water over the pygmy sperm whale, not much larger than a dolphin, with a friend and our local vet.

The vet ran a series of tests and the plan was to administer antibiotics and, when the tidal conditions were right, tow the whale out into deeper water. Meanwhile, it required constant care. A growing team of wetsuited volunteers helped throughout the day. Straddling each side, we supported the whale as we poured jugs of water to keep him wet. I was standing next to his head – and blowhole. Every few minutes, a burst of warm, rotten-egg smelling air would shoot through the hole. I quickly learned to stop inhaling and turn my head until the noxious gases dissipated.

It was a united human effort, of experts and laymen, old and young, working together with compassion for a fellow creature in distress; a combined effort to save its life. I was taken by the thought that if we all loved our fellow creatures and took action to alleviate their suffering – if all seven billion of us recognised the sentience of animals and treated them with reverence and kindness – how different our world would be. As I surveyed the group around me, my heart was enlivened by the possibilities of a better world and hope for the future of our planet.

While I rhythmically splashed water over the whale, my mind drifted back to when my relationship with animals began. I was eleven years old in a small country town. On a scorching summer's day, on my way to join a friend at the pool, I saw a string of livestock carriages sitting motionless at the railway station, crammed with hundreds of sheep. The luckier ones had their heads protruding through the steel bars, and they were panting. The less fortunate were jammed into the side panels with their legs poking awkwardly out, while those in the centre must have been suffocating.

I had seen photographs and movies about the holocaust and this seemed no different to me. I felt a deep sympathy for the sheep, although in my naivety I assumed they would soon be released into a shaded paddock with clean, fresh water. I wanted to think this was a one-off human error that would be corrected at any moment.

It was late afternoon when I returned home, cool and satisfyingly exhausted after a day at the pool. As I approached the railway station, I saw the carriages were still there, emanating the putrid smell of ammonia and manure. The sheep had been there all day, with no shade or water, their hot, crammed bodies shifting only slightly into spaces left by those who had collapsed.

Distraught, I ran to the station office in search of an adult who could help. Nobody was around. Tormented by their suffering and the realisation that I could do nothing, my only comfort was the knowledge that the sun's imminent setting would bring them some relief.

The next morning, the carriages had gone. The suffering souls had moved on, though they never left my memory.

I intrinsically knew this was wrong – that what we find abhorrent for people was acceptable for other animals. I knew, even then, that in our capacity to suffer, we are equal. At age eleven, I felt powerless to solve the problem, but I became sensitised to animal welfare issues. The more I learned about the plight of animals, the more I wanted to help them.

After university, I wanted to get as far away from the city as I could. My biophilic compass pointed me to the outback. My first job was teaching Aboriginal children in the heart of the Northern Territory. I later moved to western Queensland as a teacher at Longreach School of Distance Education. A few years later, I found myself running sheep and cattle stations with my husband. During that time, I witnessed countless incidents of abuse and apathy towards animals, incidents that had recurred unchallenged, perpetuated from one generation to the next.

One day, for example, I was helping load sheep into the bottom deck of a road train as quietly and calmly as possible. A young 'apprentice' driver was working alongside me, jabbing the sheep with an electric jigger, shouting at them and encouraging his pack of barking dogs to incite further fear. Meanwhile, on the top deck, the seasoned driver was packing the sheep into the carriage pens. One poor old ewe was particularly frightened and something went wrong. Perhaps she stood in the wrong place, or fell over. Whatever it was, the driver exploded with rage, grabbed her and hurled her off the truck like a bag of flour. She landed on the ground with a bone-breaking thump, stunned and lifeless. Meanwhile, the young assistant watched and learned.

I knew this deep-rooted cruelty and disconnection needed to change, but I didn't then know how.

'PFFFFF ...' another blast of smelly sulphuric air from the whale brought me back to the present. I looked into his big, gentle eye and felt an empathetic connection. 'What are you thinking?' I wondered. And I tried to imagine a world through his eyes, and the eyes of all animals. What we would hear if they could speak: tales of lives in polluted oceans and disappearing forests; in science laboratories, circuses, rodeos, factory farms, trucks and abattoirs.

After leaving western Queensland, I undertook a postgraduate Animal Welfare course with Monash University, and through that, I found the solution for animals I had been looking for since I was eleven. I discovered Humane Education, a discipline which promotes compassion and respect for all living things through recognising the interdependence of animals, people and ecosystems. Humane Education empowers people with the knowledge, skills and motivation to address human rights, environmental preservation and animal protection. It equips people to become 'solutionaries.'

Humane Education (HE) can break the cycle of abuse and apathy towards animals, people and the environment. The inclusion of Humane Education in our education system could create a generation of change-makers working in a new, ethical and sustainable way. Many great minds agree. According to Nelson Mandela, 'The most powerful weapon we can use to change the world is education.' Einstein observed, 'You can't fix a problem with the same kind of thinking that caused it.' Indeed, we need new ideas, new attitudes and new directions. We need to throw out the 'get more for less' model and replace it with something that makes ethical, environmental and economic sense.

Most people would prefer a world of peace, compassion and justice over a world of oppression and abuse. HE would create ethical lawyers, advocates, politicians, journalists, teachers, farmers, scientists and consumers to shape a new way of sharing our planet.

Although I came to HE as a solution for animals, I knew that they shared a common destiny with humans and our ecosystems. Dr Jane Goodall, renowned primatologist, humanitarian and UN Messenger of Peace, realised this many years ago. Jane knew that to save chimpanzees from extinction, we need to consider the needs and habitats of the people who live near chimpanzee habitats. We need to take a holistic approach. Jane is a champion solutionary. She addressed the problem by creating the Jane Goodall Institute, which operates community-centred conservation programs in Africa and a global Humane Education program which is empowering ethical young leaders in more than 130 countries. If only the program had been available when I was eleven.

My excitement about Jane Goodall's program has been enduring.

I was a volunteer for the Institute in Australia for years and currently have the honour of being its CEO. In a world fraught with despair, Jane's program gives us hope. With a critical mass working together, anything is possible.

Jane Goodall says, 'Every individual matters. Every individual has a role to play. Every individual makes a difference.' But remember, it is we who *choose* what sort of difference we make, whether it be positive or destructive. To grow good people who make positive choices, we need to inform them about critical issues, appeal to their compassion and motivate altruistic actions. We need to give them an early connection to animals, people and nature so that they care. The grandson of Mahatma Gandhi, Arun Gandhi, says education needs a triple focus – the head (knowledge), the heart (compassion) and the hands (work and action) – to create peaceful, compassionate and sustainable Earth stewards.

A wave broke across the whale and as the cold water sprayed over me I was brought back to the present and the plight of this one life. The sun was setting over the bay, the towboats had arrived and, with the support of a canvas sling, our whale was gently glided out to deeper water and the freedom of the ocean. A happy ending for one, and a reminder of the billions of other individual lives in need of our help.

....

To find out more about Natalie's work with the Jane Goodall Institute, visit the Jane Goodall Institute Australia website (www.janegoodall.org.au).

LIVING WITH TECHNOLOGY

GROWING UP IN A DIGITAL WORLD
ASSOCIATE PROFESSOR JANE BURNS

Online interaction has become the chosen method of communication for young people in the 21st century. As a society that is speeding towards an increasingly digital world, we must equip young people with the knowledge they need to protect themselves online and ensure they are adopting good online practices.

Young people are growing up in a world where technology is part of the everyday, with digital communication being fundamental to the way our society functions. Technology is with us to stay; it continues to evolve on a daily basis, and is now deeply entrenched in our work, social, family and school lives. As the parents and teachers of the younger generation we strive to be role models to the young people in our lives. Yet we often struggle to understand the role of technology in the lives of young people and as a result, may see technology as a risk. The challenge for us is to manage the risk but understand the opportunity afforded to our young people by the digital world and help them flourish.

The term 'social networking service' or SNS is used frequently these days in describing the types of programs, pages and apps young people use – but what does it actually mean? These SNS are web-based services that allow individuals to construct a public or semi-public profile within a bounded system. The use of SNS is almost universal among young people, with this demographic flocking to websites such as Facebook, Twitter, Pinterest and Tumblr to communicate and express themselves. Young people are able to establish their own networks and decide with whom they share personal information and experience. Hurdles to traditional social interaction are flattened by these social media platforms, rendering geographical location seemingly irrelevant, allowing young people with a disability to be a part of a supported community, and creating a safe space for culturally and linguistically diverse (CALD) young people to connect – all at the click of a mouse.

The internet is a powerful tool and is being widely employed to connect people with services and information. For example, using online platforms as arenas for health promotion used to be seen as purely complementary to traditional means of interaction. However, as technology has advanced and become more accessible, this mode of engagement has become intrinsic in our everyday lives. It provides an unprecedented reach, allowing not-for-profit organisations, government departments and healthcare service providers to broadcast their messages far and wide. When stigma about help-seeking, confusion about particular thoughts and feelings, and isolation prove challenging, a website is often the first port of call, with 43 per cent of young people accessing health information online (Burns et al., 2013). This further highlights the need for the provision of trusted, accurate and reliable information. The ease and confidentiality of accessing this information can be empowering for the individual, both in increasing their understanding and in encouraging their efforts to seek further professional help. Australia leads the world in the provision of youth mental health services, with ReachOut.com, eheadspace and The Butterfly Foundation Web Counselling continuing to set the standard for the e-health and e-mental health sector.

A major hurdle faced by parents and teachers is the intergenerational gap of knowledge in relation to the internet, social networking and technological advances. Most adults of today did not grow up in a world filled with smartphones, laptops and tablet devices, and consequently do not feel equipped to guide their children or students – we may not know how to set the best example.

The answer, however, is not switching to protectionist mode, but instead endeavouring to understand just how young people are using technology, and what role it plays in their lives. As parents and teachers, we must arm young people with the skills to use social networking sites and the internet in general in a responsible, considered and contributive manner – to be real 'cybercitizens' and be able to meaningfully participate in their chosen forums. We must promote the benefits of online engagement and internet usage, while appropriately addressing the risks to young people when undertaking these practices (Campbell & Robards, 2013).

Unfortunately, some young people continue to be victims of cyberbullying, negating their online experience and undermining the confidence of them and the adult guardians in their life. Both state and federal lawmakers are making moves towards legislating tough penalties for individuals proved guilty of intimidating, embarrassing, discriminating and/or threatening others online. As a society that is speeding towards an increasingly digital world, we must equip young people with the knowledge on how to protect themselves online, an understanding of these laws, and ensure they are adopting good online practices.

The line between online and offline continues to blur for the younger generations, and there continues to be less distinction made between the two – young people are living, working, learning and contributing to both of these spheres, and do not consider them to be innately separate. We want the young people in our lives to thrive and feel included, be able to contribute to society and to feel confident in doing so. The rapid uptake of SNS by young people has transformed 'communication practices, opening new spaces and processes of socialisation and impacting upon traditional social structures' (Collin et al., 2011). The online world provides the ideal space for young people to meet, form communities, share common interests, and to establish a place where they feel comfortable to express themselves. There is a level of ownership young people and their peers have of this space, just like that of a local park or shopping centre (Wiseman, 2013). By generating user-friendly hubs online, which are both accessible – including to same-sex attracted young people, young people in rural areas, Aboriginal and Torres Strait Islander young people, young people with a disability and CALD young people – and interesting to use, the internet can play a very productive role in fostering community connections, all online and not geographically bound.

Online interaction has become the chosen method of communication for young people in the 21st century. It is accessible, user-friendly, and allows individuals to express themselves by sharing their interests, likes, dislikes, and opinions to a wide audience via social media. Young people are the experts in this arena, upturning the traditional adult–child knowledge exchange – in this case, we as parents and teachers can learn from the young people in our lives. To understand each other's perspective, there must be a meaningful dialogue between the generations; one that encourages young people to share their experience and knowledge of cybersafety, while also addressing the concerns of their parents or teachers (Third et al., 2011). By continuing to learn as adults from the young people in our lives, we will help ensure that they are able to safely contribute to and learn from the ever-growing online world.

Burns, J. et al. (2013). *Game on: Exploring the impact of technologies on young men's mental health and wellbeing.* Findings from the first Young and Well National Survey. Australia, Young and Well Cooperative Research Centre.

Campbell, A. & Robards, F. (2013). *Using technologies safely and effectively to promote young people's wellbeing: A Better Practice Guide for Services.* Abbotsford, NSW Centre for the Advancement of Adolescent Health, Westmead and Young and Well Cooperative Research Centre.

Collin, P. et al. (2011). *The Benefits of Social Networking Services.* Sydney, Cooperative Research Centre for Young People, Technology and Wellbeing.

Third, A. et al. (2011). *Intergenerational Attitudes towards Social Networking and Cybersafety: A living lab.* Melbourne, Cooperative Research Centre for Young People, Technology and Wellbeing.

Wiseman, R. (2013). *Masterminds & Wingmen: Helping Our Boys Cope with Schoolyard Power, Locker-Room Tests, Girlfriends, and the New Rules of Boy World.* USA, Harmony Books.

Jane Burns is a member of the Young and Well Cooperative Research Centre, an Australia-based international research centre that unites young people with researchers, practitioners, innovators and policy-makers from over 70 partner organisations, established under the

Australian government's Cooperative Research Centres Program. The centre explores the role of technology in young people's lives, and how it can be used to improve the mental health and wellbeing of young people aged 12 to 25.

Connect with the Young and Well Cooperative Research Centre online at www.youngandwellcrc.org.au or through your preferred social network.

CYBERSAFETY: KEEPING CHILDREN SAFE ONLINE
JEREMY BLACKMAN AND SANDRA CRAIG

Cybersafety, digital citizenship, digital literacy ... most of us have heard these terms, but what do they really mean? And why are people so concerned about the risks to young people using digital technology and the internet? Is the situation really that bad?

While conversations about youth cybersafety should recognise there are opportunities as well as risks in the online world, it is reasonable to be concerned about the kinds of negative and dangerous experiences young people are exposed to online and important to have strategies to address these.

The challenge can sometimes seem insurmountable. As adults we often feel disconnected from the hyper-connected world of young people, and a common sentiment is: 'I just don't know how to help. When I grew up I never experienced what they are going through.' However, youth cybersafety issues, including cyberbullying, *can* be addressed if we increase our understanding of the issues and take advantage of the holistic, considered strategies developed by researchers and other industry experts in recent years. This chapter aims to bring these issues and solutions into sharp focus.

Cybersafety risks

Among parents, a general concern for cybersafety has been on the rise for the last few years. *Like, Post, Share: Young Australians and online privacy*, the report of a survey conducted by the Australian Communications and Media Authority in 2012, revealed 48 per cent of parents were 'very concerned' about cybersafety, while 77 per cent reported being concerned about their child's use of social networks, particularly in relation to cyberbullying and potential contact with strangers.

Teachers consistently cite mobile technologies and inappropriate online content (e.g. online pornography or aggressive content) as the biggest cybersafety issues facing children, and often express concern about the technology knowledge gap between themselves and their students (*How Teachers Are Using Technology at Home and in Their Classrooms*, 2013, Pew Research Centre).

Children and young people, both in Australia and Europe, have expressed similar concerns in studies in recent years. Unwanted attention from strangers and cyberbullying always rate highly (*Teenagers, Legal Risks and Social Networking Sites*, 2011, Monash University; EU Kids Online, *Annual Report*, 2012), while pornography and violent content risks also feature prominently.

So, inappropriate online content, cyberbullying and unwanted contact from strangers seem to be the predominant concerns. The broader issue of 'online privacy' is also a common concern, and one that is interpreted in very different ways by older and younger generations, as information-sharing practices (such as images, videos and personal details) have changed with the advent of new technologies. For example, whereas young people may believe it 'normal' to share personal photos with a wide audience, older people often believe that personal photos are only to be shared with selected family and friends.

The impact of cyberbullying

Bullying, whether online or offline, is a relationship-based problem. Its defining characteristics are a desire to hurt, humiliate, intimidate or exclude another person or group of people; an imbalance of power; and repetition.

All forms of bullying are harmful and stressful and the targets of such behaviour often feel unable to escape or get help, either at the time or later. In cases of cyberbullying, the impact can be magnified due to the 24/7 nature of digital technologies, the capacity for technology to rapidly transmit vicious content to a wide audience, and the tendency of the bullying behaviour to be more aggressive, given the physical separation between bully and target.

There is growing awareness in Australia and other parts of the world about the impact of cyberbullying, in particular its lasting negative effects. There is also concern about its increasing prevalence. In a recent study, 21 per cent of 14 to 15 year olds reported having experienced cyberbullying, with 74 per cent of those saying it had happened in the past year (ACMA, 2012). The increased use of social networking websites and mobile devices is often identified as the reason for this rising trend.

The role of digital citizenship

How do we best strike a balance between maximising the benefits of technology while safeguarding children from the harms of cyberbullying, disturbing online content and unwanted attention from strangers?

Some organisations, including schools, believe – or hope – that they can create cultural change by engaging a charismatic speaker, or implementing a short-term program. Of the latter, they are assailed with a wide range of choices from competing products, most of them claiming to be engaging, impactful and transformative.

The reality is that simplistic, one-off messages and activities are unlikely to have a lasting effect on behaviour. Cybersafety is an issue based in behaviours and relationships, and one which extends across society. For this reason, addressing the issue requires a deeper cultural change approach. The ultimate vision should be based on digital citizenship, with the recognition that we all have a part to play in becoming smart, safe and responsible digital citizens.

The solution needs to focus on settings where young people interact with technology; it needs to equip them with values consistent with an inclusive society, the skills to navigate safely, and the ability to make the most of new opportunities and possibilities.

Many of us are already making the effort to nurture good digital citizenship, but it's early days yet, and there are ways we can do this better. The following represents some practical tips to help encourage smart, safe and responsible online behaviour, whether you are a parent, a teacher or a young person.

Parents – five ways to create an eSmart home

1. *Take the time to set up your home technology in a smart and safe way*
   This includes securing wi-fi and other devices with strong passwords, using the appropriate internet filters, and regularly updating software, including antivirus software.

2. *Understand your role as a parent in keeping your children safe online*
   This includes having conversations about cybersafety with family members and young people, including setting behavioural expectations and boundaries.

3. *Know and understand the risks*
   This includes being informed about the internet and the range of digital devices your family is using and what they can do.

4. *Recognise the signs of problems and know what to do about them*
   Having a better awareness of your children's online activities through regular communication will help you spot potential issues earlier, hopefully before they escalate. Responding to issues can range from social and emotional guidance, working closely with the school (and knowing what the school's policies and procedures are), to reporting serious incidents via formal channels.

5. *Stay up-to-date and get the best out of available technologies*
   This includes developing an ongoing interest in how new technologies can benefit the lives of your family members, or at least understanding how others might genuinely appreciate them.

Schools

MacKillop College in Werribee, Victoria has initiated a very successful whole-school cybersafety program that encompasses all kinds of learning throughout the college, and engages staff, students and parents in an ongoing process.

During the first semester of each year, the Year 7 students undertake a program in their Humanities and English classes where they are provided with a chance to develop their digital literacy skills. The 'Working in our Digital Workplace' program has proven an effective way to induct new students into the values and expectations of the school, especially in regard to digital technologies.

Staff are offered a variety of professional learning models centred on technology and pedagogy, including online and face-to-face tutorials and training days, email alerts regarding the safe use of technology, and whole-staff presentations.

As an eSmart school, MacKillop College recognises the roles all members of the school community play in establishing shared attitudes and desirable behaviours regarding technology decision-making.

Based on the example of MacKillop College, a successful behaviour change program in schools would involve:

1. *A whole-of-school approach*
   Its ongoing implementation relies on a shared
   workload and involvement of all key groups in
   decision-making.
2. *Continuous review and improvement*
   It is flexible and able to adapt to changing demands
   and environments, and its effectiveness and relevance
   is regularly reviewed.
3. *It works to establish shared attitudes, not merely
   imposing 'top-down' directives*
   Compliance in any institution relies on its participants
   making decisions based on their own enduring values
   and attitudes that are supported externally.

Young people

While today's young people are generally more familiar with touch screens, wireless devices and online social networking than older people, there are some fundamental cybersafety guidelines that can serve them and hopefully protect them from the more costly mistakes that can occur when they explore and experiment in the course of learning.

1. *Privacy settings online*
    Being conscious of, and in control of privacy settings on social networking sites. This includes protecting others' privacy by always obtaining permission before uploading their content.

2. *Downloading, uploading, sharing*
    Being knowledgeable about how data/content is used on the internet, and knowing which websites are trustworthy.

3. *Ignoring, reporting, storing*
    Being aware of when difficult situations can simply be ignored, and when they require formal reporting – and what information needs to be saved as evidence.

As with parents and school communities, young people cannot take their cybersafety knowledge for granted – it needs to be maintained as the digital environment changes and new risks and opportunities emerge.

....

Jeremy Blackman and Sandra Craig work with the Alannah and Madeline Foundation, a national charity protecting children from violence and creating behavioural change in the community to address bullying and cyberbullying. The Foundation was established in memory of Alannah and Madeline Mikac, aged six and three, who, with their mother and 32 others were killed at Port Arthur, Tasmania on 28 April 1996.

The Foundation cares for children who experience or witness serious violence and develops programs designed to help prevent violence in the lives of children. It also plays an advocacy role against childhood violence. Visit the Alannah and Madeline Foundation website at www.amf.org.au to find out about their work, their programs and other resources.

THE PORNOGRAPHIC EXPERIMENT ON YOUNG PEOPLE
MELINDA TANKARD REIST

If there is any argument still to be had about whether porn impacts on young people's sexual attitudes and behaviours, then it's time to listen to young people themselves. Parents and educators need to open up safe spaces for children and young people to talk about pornography and, by contrast, healthy sexuality.

Youth worker and sexuality educator Maree Crabbe and academic and writer David Corlett interviewed 75 young people for their documentary *Love and Sex in an Age of Pornography*, shown in Australia on SBS in July and August 2013. The young people's candid disclosures show how significantly porn is influencing youth behaviour. Young men are being conditioned and shaped by messages imbibed through pornography that give them a sense of entitlement to the bodies of women and girls. Young women are under extreme pressure to give men what they want, to adopt pornified roles and behaviours and treat their bodies merely as sex aids.

The online globalisation of pornographic imagery has led to destructive ideas about sex. Healthy sexual exploration is distorted by pornographic socialisation. The importance of consent and respect has become clouded, while sexual conquest and domination is given primacy. Making love is replaced with sexual pounding. And nearly every kid knows what anal is.

Jake, 18, says of his first sexual experience at 15:

> *First time I had sex, because I'd watched so much porn I thought all chicks dig this, all chicks want this done to*

them ... all chicks love it there. So I tried all this stuff and, yeah, it turned out bad ... When a guy watches porn, he goes, 'That's hot, I want to try that ...' And they will just keep pressuring and pressuring. I've got mates who do it. They will tell you, 'Yeah, she didn't want to at first but I just kept hounding her and hounding her and finally she let me ...'

The level of disempowerment of the girls is worrying. Disconnected from their own sense of pleasure and intimacy, they often pretend to like certain acts to keep boys happy:

I think men think they'll test, that they'll see if they can do whatever they see in porno ... A past person I've been with assumed I'd enjoy something he'd seen and it almost feels hard to say no ('Kristen', age 22).

Girls, they love it in porn so maybe boys think that girls like that and ... when you love someone, you know, you're always willing to just ... make them happy. If they want to give me a pearl necklace [ejaculate on the neck] and I'm in love then I'll do it for you and I'll pretend that I like it ... And in the end ... I just became an object ... ('Sara', age 20).

Porn use becomes habitual. Malcolm, aged 16, told the BBC (BBC online news, 8 February 2007): 'It almost lodges itself into your mind, like a parasite sucking away the rest of your inner life and you kind of use it to answer everything and anything. It's a drug.'

Ninety-two per cent of boys and 61 per cent of girls aged 13 to 16 report having been exposed to pornography online (Fleming et al., 2006).

Children are growing up in the shadow of pornography. It comes to them at the click of a button. They are seeing violent pornography before even having had their first kiss. Some are becoming compulsive porn users as documented in a report in *The Age*. Porn contributes to the practice of sexual bullying and harassment as boys pressure girls to provide naked images. Twelve and 13 year old schoolgirls show me texts requesting naked images.

Porn and violence in young people

There is also rising child-on-child sexual assault. Boys are acting out what they see in pornography. Children as young as five are being treated by clinicians in Victoria, Australia, for engaging in sexual behaviour that is deemed inappropriate and/or unhealthy.

Offences by school-aged children have quadrupled in Australia in only four years according to the Australian Bureau of Statistics. The Australian Psychological Society reports adolescent boys are estimated to be responsible for about a fifth of rapes of adult women and between a third and a half of all reported sexual assaults of children.

According to a 2010 content analysis of the most popular porn, 88 per cent of scenes included acts of physical aggression and 48 per cent contained verbal aggression. In 94 per cent of cases, the aggression was directed towards women who were shown enjoying it (Reist & Bray, 2011). Boys are taught that women enjoy aggressive treatment such as being hit, choked, subject to gagging and multiple penetration. Women are expected to find this erotic.

Porn and mental health

A 2012 report of the UK Independent Parliamentary Inquiry into Online Child Protection found that exposure to porn has a negative impact on children's attitudes to sex, relationships and body image. Cross-country studies link teens' frequent consumption of porn with acceptance of sexual harassment and the idea that it is all right to hold a girl down and force her to have sex (Tankard Reist & Bray, 2011).

The Australian Medical Association says there is a strong relationship between exposure to sexually explicit material and sexual behaviour that predisposes young people to adverse sexual and mental health outcomes.

A recent report by the UK Children's Commissioner stated access and exposure to pornography are linked to children and young people's engagement in 'risky behaviours' such as engagement in sexual practices from a younger age, engagement in riskier sexual behaviours such as unprotected anal or oral sex, and the use of drugs and alcohol in sex. Young people who used pornography were more likely to report having had anal sex, sex with multiple partners and using alcohol and drugs during sex (Horvath et al., 2013).

In the report's Foreword, Sue Berelowitz, Deputy Children's Commissioner for England, sums up the findings:

> *The first year of our Inquiry ... revealed shocking rates of sexual violation of children and young people ... The Inquiry team heard children recount appalling stories about being raped by both older males and peers, often in extremely violent and sadistic circumstances, and in abusive situations that frequently continued for years ... The use of and children's access to pornography emerged as a key theme ... It was mentioned by boys in witness statements after being apprehended for the rape of a child, one of whom said it was 'like being in a porn movie'; we had frequent accounts of both girls' and boys' expectations of sex being drawn from pornography they had seen; and professionals told us troubling stories of the extent to which teenagers and younger children routinely access pornography, including extreme and violent images. We also found compelling evidence that too many boys believe that they have an absolute entitlement to sex at any time, in any place, in any way and with whomever they wish. Equally worryingly, we heard that too often girls feel they have no alternative but to submit to boys' demands, regardless of their own wishes.*

The experiences of young people, combined with a growing body of disturbing research findings, show we are conducting a never before seen experiment on youth sexual development by allowing unrestricted exposure to pornography. But one small sign of hope is that young people still have a desire for authentic intimacy and love: for something better than porn offers. As Joel says in the SBS film: 'It is all about being close to that person and showing them how much you love them ...'

Managing the risks

Parents and educators need to open up safe spaces for children and young people to talk about pornography and, by contrast, healthy sexuality. While it is hard for many parents to raise the topic of sex with their kids, if they don't, someone else may fill the vacuum and it may not be someone who supports the parents' desires and values for their children. Conversations should emphasise what it means to be in a loving relationship – if possible, modelled by the parents themselves – and how sex fits into this picture.

Computers should be in a public place in the house, with filtering software installed as well as a program that filters and tracks internet activity. Parents should learn how technology works, in order to understand the risks that need to be managed. A great site for this is: www.commonsensemedia.org.

Schools should not tolerate sexual harassment, sexual joking, inappropriate touching, and downloading of porn on phones and tablets in the school ground.

Despite the evident need for young people to be supported in dealing with the many issues raised by pornography, there are few classroom-based resources on this subject, though some are under development. New programs should be designed with respectful relationships as the starting point, not just 'sex education.' Young people want content based on their real lives and experiences – information that empowers and equips them to make healthy decisions about their sexuality.

BBC News: news.bbc.co.uk/2/hi/uk_news/magazine/6336509.stm.

Fleming, M.J. et al. (2006). 'Safety in Cyberspace', *Youth and Society*, *38*, pp. 135–54.

Horvath, M.A.H. et al. (2013). *'Basically ... porn is everywhere' – A Rapid Evidence Assessment on the Effects that Access and Exposure to Pornography has on Children and Young People*. A report published by the UK Children's Commissioner, p. 36.

Tankard Reist, M. & Bray, A. (eds) (2011). *Big Porn Inc: Exposing the harms of the global pornography industry*. Spinifex Press, Melbourne.

Visit Melinda's site (www.melindatankardreist.com) to find out about her book *Big Porn Inc* along with details of her work and other publications.

FLOURISHING AT SCHOOL

POSITIVE EDUCATION: AN INTENTIONAL FOCUS ON WELLBEING
JUSTIN ROBINSON

Positive Education establishes a common language for the school community to explore and nurture wellbeing; it teaches the skills of wellbeing to all members of the community and establishes a culture which promotes and enables flourishing.

I have no doubt that all the major stakeholders in education desire wellbeing for all students in all schools in all countries. Inherently we understand that an individual's wellbeing is the foundation on which success in life is built. If students are able to develop healthy levels of personal wellbeing then they will be more likely to achieve their academic potential, more likely to establish supportive relationships, more likely to make a meaningful contribution to their community and more likely to lead a fulfilling life.

At Geelong Grammar School we strongly believe that personal wellbeing is each student's right and that as a school community we must endeavour to make wellbeing accessible and available to each student. This commitment to our students has become known as Positive Education, which has an intentional focus on cultivating wellbeing in students and also, importantly, in teachers.

The idea of Positive Education is to assist students to flourish, which we define for our students at Geelong Grammar School as the powerful combination of 'feeling good and doing good.' By extension, a key objective of Positive Education is to promote mental health and prevent mental illness. Professor Corey Keyes of Emory University argues that the absence of mental illness does not indicate the presence of mental health: he classifies complete mental health as a state in which individuals are free of mental illness and are flourishing. Research supports our intuition that flourishing individuals function markedly better than all others.

Positive Education is a whole-school approach to exploring skills and abilities for flourishing in life (skills such as identifying and using one's character strengths, understanding the importance of positive emotions, and promoting meaning and purpose in one's life), and skills for coping with life (such as resilience, mindfulness and acceptance). Since 2009, Geelong Grammar School has been implementing Positive Education across each of its four campuses. The framework we use is 'Live It, Teach It and Embed It.'

Live It

Our first priority is in providing all staff (teaching and non-teaching) with a clear understanding of the key concepts of Positive Education. Staff participate in a three-day Introduction to Positive Education course held at the start of each school year, and attend a number of refresher workshops each term. We see it as vitally important for staff to explore and address their own wellbeing so that they have a personal, felt experience of the benefits and impact of Positive Education and are thus able to role-model and 'live' its tenets.

Teach It

Geelong Grammar School has developed an Applied Framework for Positive Education, which provides an empirically informed roadmap for how positive psychology can be applied and embedded in schools. Positive Education is explicitly taught in all year levels from Years 5 to 10. More than 150 hours of contact teaching time are dedicated to exploring the skills students require to live a flourishing life, sending a strong message to our community that wellbeing is important.

Domains addressed and explored in Positive Education include Positive Relationships; Positive Emotions; Positive Health; Positive Engagement; Positive Accomplishment and Positive Purpose. Within each of these domains are topics, skills and activities designed to assist students and teachers to nurture both their own wellbeing and the wellbeing of others. A summary of our model for Positive Education, including detailed research summaries for each of the domains, can be found on the school's website.

As all staff are trained in Positive Education and all academic departments are charged with the responsibility of making relevant links to wellbeing within their curricula, students are exposed to Positive Education concepts and language on a regular basis.

Embed It

The tenets of Positive Education are embedded in every aspect of school life, from school assemblies and chapel services through to our co-curricular program and staff appraisal system. The Positive Education Department is responsible for a range of school-wide practices, including Random Acts of Kindness, What Went Well boards, meeting protocols, story sharing, staff health and wellbeing initiatives and community celebrations.

A common language of wellbeing spreads throughout our school community as key terms intrinsic to Positive Education are used in conversation among students and staff: character strengths, mindsets, resilience, mindfulness, active constructive responding, flow, savouring, thinking traps, icebergs. Hearing this shared understanding and common language, a visitor to the school remarked that Positive Education was 'in the water' at Geelong Grammar.

Positive Education and positive psychology

A key tenet of Positive Education is that a student's individual wellbeing is critically important. A flourishing student is engaging in their learning, contributing positively to their community and nurturing many healthy relationships. Positive Education provides strategies to get the best out of all life's situations, from exercising resilience when facing adversity to striving for future goals with realistic hope and optimism when things are going well. In a time when the prevalence of depression and anxiety are on the rise in adolescents, education must endeavour to prevent mental illness and promote mental wellness.

In its intentional focus on teaching and embedding wellbeing skills to enable students and communities to thrive, Positive Education can be understood as the application of positive psychology in educational contexts. Positive psychology is the scientific study of the factors which contribute to living a full and meaningful life. It is a psychological science and practice that is as concerned with strength as it is with weakness, with making the lives of all people fulfilling as with healing those suffering from illness.

Geelong Grammar School was fortunate to have been introduced to Positive Education by Dr Martin Seligman when he visited us in 2008. Since this time, the school has embraced the responsibility of developing and promoting the field. Many leading psychologists and educators, both nationally and internationally, have contributed to the school's Positive Education program and we feel that our community is significantly closer, kinder, more resilient and healthier due to our whole-school approach to wellbeing.

Bringing Positive Education to your school
We encourage all schools to broaden their focus on student wellbeing by addressing 'what's strong' as well as 'what's wrong.' Taking a strengths-based approach to student and staff wellbeing as well as school culture can lead to exciting growth and development.

Schools are encouraged to carry out an audit of their wellbeing offerings and map their various programs and activities onto the key domains of Positive Education: Relationships, Emotions, Health, Engagement, Accomplishment and Purpose. No doubt many, if not all, schools already have activities and programs in place which align with the goals of Positive Education. Therefore, most schools are already implementing at least some elements of Positive Education.

Schools are urged to weave wellbeing initiatives through everything they do. They should provide staff with a strong understanding of the concepts of Positive Education and adopt a sustainable approach to nurturing staff wellbeing. To increase the effectiveness of Positive Education, schools should prioritise a dedicated subject in the timetable devoted to teaching the skills of wellbeing. Schools must also look carefully at their current school culture to ensure the environment is conducive to wellbeing.

Hope for the future

There remains much work still to be done in the field of Positive Education. Further longitudinal research needs to be carried out on diverse groups of students to determine which skills and activities best promote sustainable wellbeing for which types of students. Additional curriculum materials must be developed which engage students in truly getting to know and understand themselves and others. Training in the core concepts of Positive Education must become more readily accessible for teachers in all schools, while all teachers should be encouraged to collaborate and share materials which are working within their schools.

Positive Education provides us with great reasons to be optimistic about the future health and wellbeing of our students and children. Schools and teachers are doing excellent work in creating activities and programs which prevent ill-being and promote wellbeing. I anticipate this will lead to a significant decline in many of the troubling statistics on adolescent health, and also a rise in student engagement and purpose. At Geelong Grammar School, our stated focus is 'learning to flourish.' We continue to find great meaning in our work and look forward to sharing our learning with the wider educational community as we maintain our commitment to holding wellbeing at the core of education.

To find out more about Geelong Grammar School and their pioneering approach to Positive Education, visit their school website (www.ggs.vic.edu.au).

PUTTING THE CHILD AT THE CENTRE: A WHOLE-SCHOOL APPROACH

PRINCIPALS AUSTRALIA INSTITUTE ON BEHALF OF KIDSMATTER PRIMARY

The KidsMatter framework provides Australian primary schools with a whole-school approach to the development of the social, emotional and mental health and wellbeing of children.

Current reform agendas concerning Australian schools do little to address the issue of nurturing the social capital of our young people. Schools are facing challenges around standardised curriculum, demanding accountability frameworks, compliance-based funding and differing state and federal agendas – all within the context of a world view that sees competition as the means of bringing about best practice in schools.

The development of the whole child is at risk of being moved to the margins of educative policy, rather than being at the centre of it. Most who work in schools struggle with the paradox this creates. This chapter asks how we can best deal with the plethora of political imperatives imposed on us, and at the same time minister to the complex, life-impacting needs of students and their families.

The KidsMatter framework, fully funded by the Australian Department of Health and Ageing, provides Australian primary schools with a whole-school approach to developing the social, emotional and mental health and wellbeing of children. Its goal is to support the school to establish the conditions (culture, ethos, relationships, values, partnerships, social and emotional skills curriculum) which maximise the opportunities for children to flourish. Those who work in schools would be aware that these are also the conditions within which learning is optimised.

KidsMatter takes the view that the child's sense of self is influenced by three domains: their family, their school, and the community in which they live. These domains interact with each other and the individual biological and psychological predisposition of the child to create a sense of self. This sense of self is played out in a range of settings, one of which is school.

KidsMatter pedagogy is grounded in the principles of *promotion, prevention and early intervention*. It adopts a whole-school approach to optimising the social, emotional and mental health of children. It looks at factors that increase the risk of children developing poor mental health and, more importantly, the factors that reduce the risk, the so-called protective factors. KidsMatter invites schools to look at ways in which they can surround the child with as many protective factors as possible – at school, at home and in the community.

KidsMatter has been developed collaboratively by the Principals Australia Institute, the Australian Psychological Society and beyondblue, with funding from the Australian Government Department of Health and beyondblue.

A whole-school approach

KidsMatter recognises the experience, intellect, passion and commitment that thrive in schools. It does not presume to give schools a universal answer because it recognises that universal answers to complex problems do not generally work. Rather, KidsMatter poses issues for schools to consider in their local context, with their community. Many a staff library is full of discarded one-off programs that, at some time, were seen as the panacea to all manner of needs.

Those who work in schools know that establishing a genuine whole-school approach to anything is a complex process that takes time and dedication. Effective approaches have to consider often competing assumptions about:
- vision and purpose
- culture, values and climate

- mutual and ad-hoc adaptation
- variability and uniformity
- shared world views and individuals' mental models.

When a school adopts the KidsMatter framework it begins by forming an Action Team to guide the process across the school on behalf of the whole school community. One cycle of the KidsMatter journey takes up to two years as it focuses on allowing the school time to make sense of the information provided within its unique context. It is not a 'one size fits all' approach. Effective whole-school change is enhanced when it is set within a strategic, process-rich context. This approach considers four elements: setting the climate, exploring what could be possible, implementation, and embedding in a sustainable way.

1. Setting the climate
To begin, the focus is on the use of persuasion, influence and dialogue as a means of creating a groundswell of interest in exploring KidsMatter to support the social, emotional and mental wellbeing of children. This is an important time to engage and listen to multiple perspectives and to ensure all voices are heard. It is also a good time to look at any existing data or information the school has. The intent is to build a picture of the current situation.

In this initial time, 'sowing seeds' is important. This can take several forms: occasional articles in pigeonholes; wellbeing as a discussion point in performance development meetings; a ten-minute wellbeing component to each staff meeting; articles for school newsletters, to name a few. In the words of a school principal:

> *We thought it was important to have a philosophy that would fit with the positive ways we worked with children in our classrooms. We wanted to focus on resilience and it was clear that if we introduced KidsMatter, it would be more than buying a kit and using it in the classroom. It would help students to explore and understand their feelings.*

> *At a briefing, we introduced the concept. Staff were enthusiastic about it, and within a short time, time was set aside for training in Components 1 and 2. It*

*was essential to get everyone on board at the start, and
parents were informed about KidsMatter through the
newsletter. Four parents responded to the invitation to
join the Action Team.*

2. Picturing what could be

This is the time spent exploring the desired outcome or vision for
how things could be, and it is not just a one-off process; it can take
place at regular intervals. It is important that this sense of what we
are all aiming for is articulated in a way that allows for emergent or
unplanned needs. Articulating the vision clearly and using this as a
focus for change is essential for embedding the commitment to the
social, emotional and mental wellbeing of children in a sustainable
manner. A school guidance counsellor explains:

*At the beginning of the year the art teacher arranges a
large canvas for the representation of the staff vision.
The staff can draw and write ideas about the agreed
vision for the year ahead. This approach to developing
a vision is replicated in each classroom and taught
alongside a unit about the values and principles that are
important in the school.*

Time is spent mapping the steps needed to move from the
current reality to the desired scenario. The KidsMatter staff and
parents survey tools are useful in this needs analysis process. It
is also a great time to use an appreciative planning process – one
which focuses on what is working well and explores how to apply
successes to classroom practice as well as cross-curricula and policy
domains of the school. KidsMatter has a 'How does KidsMatter
build upon what we are already doing' tool to map existing practice
so that it can be used to inform strategic planning. A school principal
describes this in action:

*Parents were generally positive in their responses to
the survey for Component 1. The results confirmed the
approach that staff felt they promoted – that students
are the centre of their actions. However, the school also
identified some areas that would improve the sense of*

community and belonging. One example was to find a way to present student artwork in the school. Now, in the room where parents are interviewed for enrolment, there is an exhibition of student paintings and drawings, which is changed every few weeks. Another example is the placement of a tub with toys for smaller children to play with while their parents participate in enrolment interviews.

3. Implementing

By now, the rationale for using the KidsMatter framework to guide practice is clear and supported. Facilitated shared learning, provided by KidsMatter and the School Action Team, is an important part of this phase. It is important that all staff have the opportunity to learn about and engage with new materials and ideas. The role of school leaders in developing a climate for professional learning is vital during this phase, when the challenge is to look at the lessons learned and to use them to inform practice.

Using a plan–do–review cycle is a useful approach during implementation. KidsMatter takes the view that change needs to begin with small steps to change and improvement. Small first steps are lower risk in that they involve small changes; they give confidence to staff because they allow some control over the pace of the program implementation.

4. Embedding in a sustainable manner

Here the emphasis is on embedding identified good practice into the everyday world of the school and continually reviewing practices in light of the ever-changing school community and its needs. This is where the desired scenario or vision becomes reality. The school has undertaken all KidsMatter professional learning, has tried different ideas, analysed what worked and used this to inform future practice. The learning that arises from this process is then used to influence whole-school culture, capacity, systems and governance practices.

Discussions about student wellbeing and mental health are a natural part of practices occurring in the classroom, within the school and within the larger school community. The focus is on KidsMatter becoming a 'way of being' across the whole school. A classroom teacher describes the process:

*We'll revisit the ideas and make sure our resources are
up-to-date. We'll continue to give information through
the 'dripping tap' process. We've made KidsMatter
Primary our own and we're helping to build up resilience
in our students. The Action Team will keep KidsMatter
Primary on the agenda even after completing Component 4.
They view it as a learning continuum in promoting the
school's role in supporting students' mental health and
wellbeing. They will review and evaluate directions as
the needs of the staff, students and community change.*

Deep change or surface change

The incredibly busy world of schools can sometimes create a predisposition to leap immediately into *who–what–when* planning. In some instances this can be a highly appropriate and effective strategy to use. However, when it becomes the automatic default planning strategy, then deep meaningful change is at risk.

The KidsMatter framework encompasses the time it takes to bring about whole-school change in a meaningful, participatory and sustainable manner. This approach allows schools the time to nurture the dispositions and culture of their setting, in order to make child-centredness a natural part of all that they do. KidsMatter holds the view that this is the essence of sustainable, deep change. A head of junior school sums it up:

*What's different about KidsMatter? All sorts of
materials sit on shelves from previous programs. But the
KidsMatter framework allows us to develop an approach
to student wellbeing that we can tailor – it is not a one
size fits all. It's not a program but a 'framework' for the
purpose of supporting students and their mental health.*

To find out more about KidsMatter Primary visit their website
(www.kidsmatter.edu.au/primary).

To find out more about Principals Australia Institute (PAI) visit www.pai.edu.au.
PAI provides quality professional learning, leadership development and support to
principals and school leaders.

AN EVIDENCE-BASED WHOLE-SCHOOL STRATEGY TO POSITIVE EDUCATION
DR MATHEW WHITE

For wellbeing to be undertaken at an institutional level we need schools to create measurable wellbeing systems rather than only focusing on wellbeing programs. Experience is showing us that a whole-school approach will have the greatest impact and involve more members of the school's teaching, parent and student community.

One of the leading psychologists in the field of wellbeing, Christopher Peterson, considers that strengths (elements that are working well) and wellbeing are cultivated not only within individual students but at the collective level, so that an institution itself could be said to have 'moral character.' So should schools embed wellbeing as a key goal in strategic planning in the same way they do mathematics or reading?

Established in 1847, St Peter's College in Adelaide, an independent Anglican boys school (K–12, enrolment 1334), is one of Australia's oldest schools. It has adopted a systems-wide wellbeing and strengths approach to teaching, learning and pastoral care, where the focus is not on changing the behaviour, emotions and cognitions of a single individual, but on enhancing those of the whole school, students and staff.

St Peter's College has adopted Martin Seligman's PERMA model of wellbeing. Seligman, the founder of the positive psychology movement, defines wellbeing in terms of five elements: positive emotion, engagement, relationships, meaning and accomplishment – forming the acronym PERMA. The model provides a framework that facilitates open discussion with students, parents, alumni and other key members of the school's community, and offers a way to talk about the school in teacher appraisal systems and student behaviour management.

PERMA also provides an ideal framework in which to develop evidence-based Positive Education, delivering lessons that have been scientifically demonstrated to have an impact on student wellbeing. Such classes include the applied skills of self-regulation, self-awareness, optimism, mental agility and strengths of character. These lessons are embedded in a whole-school strategy and the results are measured in order to improve the whole school's wellbeing, not just that of a handful of students.

At the heart of education at St Peter's College is the shaping of character and understanding and promoting wellbeing. This is not to diminish the value we place on academic mastery, but rather to emphasise that the gaining of wisdom is our true goal.

How do school communities work with parents and teachers to improve the way they look after students? Based on our experience, we caution against searching for a 'one size fits all' approach to wellbeing that only considers the classroom. Our collaboration with leading psychologists from the UK, the US and Australia suggests that a whole-school approach will have a much greater and sustainable impact and involve more members of the school's community.

Teachers and parents together need to invest in the deeper thinking of how to grow wellbeing across their community programs so that they become part of a unified whole with the potential for a long-term impact on school culture.

It is critical that the most senior school leaders are intimately involved with the creation and development of a whole-school approach because wellbeing is the concern of everyone. As we shape character in Positive Education classes and activities, we equip our boys to use knowledge and understanding based on their experiences and values. Each element of a St Peter's College education is important in achieving wellbeing. Sport, music, drama and outdoor education are as much about teamwork, perseverance, commitment, courage and fairness as they are about fitness, relaxation and adventure. Community service is about selflessness,

Chapel feeds their souls and the House provides a home where a boy is cherished, loved and understood.

We have found that adopting wellbeing as a strategic goal has been a key driver to building greater staff capability and unlocking the strengths of student culture.

Schools need to take account of a multitude of different strands in the process of making wellbeing an integral facet of their school communities. Here are seven that we found important at St Peter's College:

1. *Leadership and vision.* There must be a clear vision of wellbeing established by the most senior members of the school team and shared with parents and staff.

2. *Strategy and management.* A clear structure, set of policies, procedures and processes are needed to manage the introduction of wellbeing programs and measure their efficacy. This needs to come from the highest level of decision-making in the school, no less than the way a school would consider its finances.

3. *Community partnerships.* For schools to reflect the PERMA framework, they must become the focus of activating hubs for community wellbeing and mental health. However, schools cannot do this important work alone. We need to open our doors and engage in more community partnerships, including students, parents and key thinkers.

4. *Measurement.* An evidence-based approach is critical. We learn from the results of measurement, which has the capacity to develop learning and teaching outcomes. Schools should determine how to measure wellbeing consistent with the theoretical framework they have adopted. Measurement also aligns well with current advances in education.

5. *Knowledge transfer.* Schools need to develop their own teacher-friendly PERMA methods specific to their culture to capture curriculum ideas that can be trialled and disseminated across the school quickly and easily.

6. *Interventions*. Schools should adopt evidence-based programs that clearly align with their vision, mission and goals as an institution and are aligned with the core values of the institution.
7. *Communications*. Schools should work well in advance to develop the appropriate communications to explain to key members of the school's community why, how and what they are doing and demonstrate that they are committed to the science of wellbeing.

Developing our evidence-based whole-school approach to wellbeing represented an evolution in policy and practice from our traditional pastoral model. The process significantly enhanced our House system, which had remained relatively unchanged since the 1920s. Traditional pastoral models have been based on a school-masterly approach to wellbeing. In the PERMA framework, staff are trained to have a more sophisticated understanding of the elements and skills that are able to lead students to flourish. At St Peter's College our wellbeing strategy was to be achieved by three objectives:

1. Implement a world-class, evidence-based and dynamic wellbeing framework.
2. Ensure all staff embrace wellbeing as central to their role and responsibilities.
3. Develop St Peter's College as a centre of excellence for world's best practice in wellbeing.

For wellbeing to take hold at an institutional level we need measurable wellbeing systems rather than focusing on Positive Education programs alone. By measuring wellbeing we make visible what might otherwise be a fuzzy and invisible part of school life, and we can then develop strategies and goals around it. For example in measuring wellbeing we might discover that 'meaning' and 'connection with school' are low, whereas 'accomplishment' is high. A transparent wellbeing measure will enable school leaders to develop innovative ways to boost students' level of meaning and improve relationships.

Until educational policy writers and administrators realise what great teachers instinctively know – that a child's character is as important as their intellect – we argue that wellbeing and character strengths should be systematically adopted across the school to bridge the gap between home and school.

....

Visit the St Peter's College website to find out more about their work in Positive Education (www.stpeters.sa.edu.au).

SURVIVING YEAR TWELVE
DR MICHAEL CARR-GREGG

*We create too much hype about the final years of school
and we need to put this in the context of everything else.
Ideally there should be a chorus of adults telling students
that whatever the outcome, their life will still be worth
living – their performance in Year 12 is only a measure
of their ability in an exam at a specific point in time, not
their future success.*

According to the 2012 Mission Australia Youth Survey, coping
with stress, school and study problems remain major concerns for
respondents. Research reported in Melbourne's *Age* in 2006 reveals
that going through Year 12 can increase rates of depression and
anxiety. In 2008, the *Australian Psychologist* reported increased
suicidal thoughts among Year 12 students (McGraw, 2008) and
according to the *Sydney Morning Herald* website in 2003, there is
even evidence for increased suicide. In particular, the fear of failure
and the apparent lack of prospects for those with poor results in
Year 12 were identified as major stressors for many young people.
As well as managing school, many were also trying to cope with
work, family and social commitments. The cumulative effect of
these demands appears to be leaving many young people feeling
besieged and struggling to cope. This chapter offers parents and
teachers some skills and strategies to help young people on their
Year 12 journey.

Put the year in perspective
Are they ready? If they are going to take the Year 12 journey, it's
important that they *want* to. The final year adventure doesn't suit

all of us, and not everyone will embark on it at the same time in their lives. If they feel that the time isn't right for them, or that they have a burning passion to do something other than study, then rather than talk them out of it, encourage them instead to chat with their school careers counsellor and find out what their options are (e.g. TAFE, a job, travel, part-time study, an apprenticeship). Remember that there are many ways to get to where you want. Arguing never achieves anything, as the old saying has it, 'Never wrestle with a pig in the mud, because you both get dirty – and the pig loves it.'

Set the tone from the start. The media and those around us can spread a lot of doom and gloom about Year 12, adding a heap of pressure to an already huge year. So a key message about the final year should be that it is an important year in their lives, but it is not the most important year. It is just another stage in a student's career and the sun and the moon and the stars do not revolve around what happens at the end of it. It's important to keep things in perspective, and remind them that they are *not* their ATAR (Australian Tertiary Admission Rank) score.

Looking after themselves

Eat smarter. Consider their brain a high-powered computer – they can't expect it to function without recharging the battery! Pigging out on empty kilojoules like pizza, lollies and energy drinks won't help them study. Eating smart can increase performance, strengthen their immune system and help them cope with stress. Eating breakfast will help boost their brain-power, while munching on 'brain food' like eggs, lean protein, raw nuts, berries, low-fat cheese and avocado will fire up those neurons! Low GI carbohydrates and nutritional supplements like fish oil or flaxseed will boost memory and performance. Don't forget every cell in the body requires energy and yes, iron is needed for making haemoglobin, the red pigment that carries oxygen to cells. Their brain doesn't know (or care) where its iron comes from. The iron in seafood, poultry, legumes, vegetables or grains will do nicely. Zinc is a vital part of brain cells and assists in growth and repair and the top sources, by far, are oysters and mussels. But they'll also get plenty from any other kind of seafood, or chicken, legumes, rolled oats and other cereals, dairy products and nuts. Finally don't forget vitamin B12 which is needed for electrical impulses to be transmitted along nerve fibres and comes from chicken, fish, milk, cheese, yoghurt or eggs. Check out www.brainrules.net to find out more. Make sure they drink plenty of water to keep themselves hydrated. Dehydration is a common cause of headaches and procrastination in Year 12s.

Exercise. Year 12 students often feel there is no time to include exercise in their routine, but getting active can actually increase their performance – making it an essential study tool. The human brain evolved under conditions of almost constant motion. As a result the optimal environment for processing information would include motion. Exercise improves cognition because exercise increases oxygen flow into the brain, which reduces brain-bound free radicals – an increase in oxygen is always accompanied by a lift in mental sharpness. It is also great for burning up adrenaline and reducing muscle tension, which can result from stress and school pressure. If they are new to exercise, start gradually and build up to a goal of 30 minutes of cardiovascular exercise (running, bike riding, swimming, team sports, etc.) three times a week. Try a range of activities and find something they enjoy. Consider incorporating 10 minutes of exercise in study breaks, like throwing a basketball, running up stairs or running on the spot to re-energise their mind and de-stress their body. Smartphone exercise apps like Couch to 5K can be obtained from Apple's iTunes online store. A session should take 20 or 30 minutes, three times a week. That just happens to be the same amount of moderate exercise recommended by numerous studies for optimum fitness.

Stress and anxiety. Moderate levels of stress can be useful in keeping them motivated – without it we would find it hard to stay awake! However, during Year 12 they may find their stress levels rising into the critical zone, causing a dramatic decline in performance. Chronic low levels of stress over time can also have a negative impact on their bodies, memory, and immune system, so it's important to find ways to keep stress at bay. Proven strategies include relaxation, getting organised and managing time (make a list of activities and prioritise), connecting with others (talk about their worries, laugh, be positive), and listening to their body's needs (e.g. sleep, get comfortable, know their own limits).

Relaxation. Psychologists often say that young people can't experience feelings of relaxation and tension at the same time. Learning how to relax is a skill (like riding a bike), and like any skill gets better with practice. Learning the art of relaxation is particularly helpful for the final school year, when stress can build up. Anxiety and tension causes unpleasant physical symptoms including headache, backache, and tight chest. Relaxation techniques can counteract the effect of stress on the body. Controlled breathing exercises involve slow, regular breathing (six-second in-breath followed by six-second out-breath) and are useful to combat panic and anxiety. Try a state-of-the-art, free smartphone app like Smiling Mind (smilingmind.com.au) which is modern meditation for young people.

Sleep. Sleep is food for the brain. According to research reported by the Sleep Foundation and many other sleep research labs, sleep is essential to their wellbeing, as significant as the air you breathe, the water you drink and the food you eat. Biological sleep patterns swing towards later times for both sleeping and waking during adolescence, meaning it is natural to not be able to fall asleep before 11 pm. Teens need about 9¼ hours of sleep each night to function best (for some, 8½ hours is enough). Most teens do not get enough sleep: one study found that only 15 per cent reported sleeping 8½ hours on school nights. Did you know that just one less hour of sleep can reduce alertness the next day by 25 per cent? Or that if they reduce their sleep to just six hours per night, their immunity to viral infection is reduced by up to 50 per cent? Stats like these show how important sleep is for Year 12 students to stay healthy and focused. Encourage them to try the following tips to optimise their zzzzs.

- Go to bed and wake up at the same time every day – this will help regulate their body clock.
- Dim the lights in their environment at least half an hour before they go to bed.

- Limit social media, TV and gadgets so that they wind up at least 90 minutes before bed. The lights from their electronics will keep them awake, and their friends' updates are totally distracting!
- Relax before bed – have a bath, read a book or a magazine.
- Exercise in the afternoon – it will make them tired by bedtime.
- Avoid stimulants – limit coffee, cola and energy drink use to before noon.
- Keep good 'sleep hygiene' – limit noise or distractions, keep their room dark and cool, wake up to natural light.
- Use a smartphone app like SleepBot to monitor their sleep.

Managing study

Study smart, not hard! The following tips will help them study smarter, not longer.

- *Use mind maps.* Mind maps show the links between key concepts. Visit buzan.com.au to find out more. The relative importance of each idea is clearly indicated by how near it is to the centre, which clearly features the main idea. The links between key concepts will be immediately obvious from their proximity and connection to one another. The brain works primarily with key concepts that it links and integrates. Mind maps work in the same way, meaning that recall and review will be faster and more effective. There are two types of mind mapping: paper-based and computer-based, but both follow the same core idea of starting from the centre of the page or screen with one topic and breaking it down into sub-categories using branches, colours and other visual support. Paper-based mind maps are quick to create. Students don't need a computer or internet access, and they can easily add their own drawings. But these can also easily get lost, accidently placed in the bin, or chewed by the dog. This is avoided using software like mindmeister.com.

- *Set goals.* Setting clear, attainable goals gives them the clarity and energy to reach the outcome they want. Encourage them to write goals down, discuss them with teachers, family members and friends, and make a step-by-step action plan they can put into place to achieve them.

- *Know their learning style.* We all learn differently – some learn best through print (reading and writing), or through aural (listening), interactive (discussing ideas), visual (observation), haptic (touch), kinaesthetic (body movement), or olfactory (smell and taste) means. Parents should encourage them to incorporate their favoured learning style into their study routine to help them learn more, faster.

- *Utilise resources.* Encourage students to think of their teachers as mini Yodas (you know, from *Star Wars*) – kind of wrinkly but a great source of knowledge! They should utilise them. A Yoda can explain how to tackle practice exams from previous years, using similar questions to actual exams, and study guides to help with revision.

- *Beat procrastination.* They can beat time-wasting by breaking down assignments into manageable tasks, sticking to a work plan, challenging negative self-talk (try MoodKit) and rewarding themselves for each mini-success. Try the smartphone app iProcrastinate to stay on track.

Staying on track

Motivation. Remind students of their goals and reasons for doing Year 12. Get them to write them down on an index card and put it where they will be reminded frequently (e.g. on their computer mat).

Planning and supports. Encourage them to manage their time in advance, and enlist a friend or relative to assist. Good habits include keeping a timetable, writing a 'to-do' list every day, remembering to balance study time with rest and recreation. Year 12 is a great year to wean themselves from reality TV and get into the habit of keeping phone calls short.

Watch out for things that could derail them. Sometimes life gets in the way of study. Here are a number of common problems and how to deal with them.

- *Part-time work.* Research reported at Isay.edu.au shows that Year 12 students can combine school and part-time work with minimal impact on their study if the work hours are modest (no more than 10–15 hours a week). Interestingly, students engaging in part-time work show a stronger orientation towards work than study.

- *Depression.* Depression is a problem for between 5 and 20 per cent of Year 12 students. Be aware of the signs and symptoms of depression, and if you are concerned they should be encouraged to speak with a trusted adult or GP. They can ring the Kids Helpline on 1800551800 or log on to eheadspace or check out online resources at youthbeyondblue.com. Depression is common but treatable; it shouldn't be ignored.

- *Social media.* Some eye-opening stats if you have a social-media junkie: research shows that students who use social media sites while studying (even if only in the background) get 20 per cent lower grades than students who don't. The rare non-users of Facebook were also found to study a whopping 88 per cent longer outside class. Limiting their social networking to outside study hours will give them a huge lift towards final-year success. If they are struggling to stay away, there are some computer programs that can help. Cold Turkey for PCs is a free program they can use to temporarily block themselves from popular social media sites, addicting websites and games (available at getcoldturkey.com). 'Self-control' for Mac users is available at selfcontrolapp.com.

- *Problems at school or home.* Pressure from parents, teachers, bullying can happen in any year of school and can be too big to handle alone. Encourage them to talk to a student welfare co-ordinator, a trusted adult, or an online support service for advice and solutions.
- *Binge drinking and drugs.* Partying hard will seriously affect their productivity. If they have been using alcohol or other substances on a recreational basis, cutting down in Year 12 is a really good idea. Marijuana is particularly unhelpful and if they can't stop, they should seek professional support, available online at clearyourvision.org.au.

Special study hints for Year 12s

- Chew gum while studying – Dr A. Scholey has shown this can help concentration and memory.
- Try clenching your fist when trying to memorise important lists.
- Form a study group in which students explain things aloud. By speaking and listening to one another, students often improve the ability to remember information on test day.
- Cramming information in hour after hour is an inefficient way to study. Instead, short bursts followed by a break is reported to be a better system.
- Find a calm, comfortable regular study spot, to help get in the mood to revise.

Carskadon, M.A., et al. (1997). 'An Approach to Studying Circadian Rhythms of Adolescent Humans,' *Journal of Biological Rhythms, 12(3)*, pp. 278–89.

Gough, D. & Edwards, H. (2006). 'Pressure takes big toll on students'. *The Age,* 16 April.

McGraw, K. et al. (2008). 'Family, peer and school connectedness in final year secondary school students'. *Australian Psychologist, 43(1)*, pp. 27–37.

Mission Australia Youth Survey (2012). www.youthleadership.org.au.

Scholey, A. (2004). 'Chewing gum and cognitive performance: a case of a functional food with function but no food?', *Appetite, 43(2)*, pp. 215–16.

Sydney Morning Herald website: www.smh.com.au/articles/2003/01/23/1042911493790.html.

Youth Leadership survey: www.youthleadership.org.au/listing/20120607/mission-australia-2012-youth-survey.

Find out more about Michael and his work supporting adolescent mental health by visiting his website (www.michaelcarr-gregg.com.au).

ON EDUCATION
JANE ELLIOTT

I didn't really become an educator until 1968 when, the day after Martin Luther King Jr was killed, I used the blue-eyed, brown-eyed exercise in discrimination in my classroom with 26 third grade nine year olds. That day, I learned more than I taught, and more than I had ever learned in a college classroom.

My work is that of a lifelong educator who has little time for standardised testing and constant evaluation. So, 'Abandon hope, all ye who enter here.' Now that you've been warned, whether you continue to read this is entirely up to you. While I am willing to be held responsible for what I write, I accept no responsibility whatsoever for your reactions to my ramblings.

The topic is education. The word 'educate' comes from the root *duc, duce-*, which means lead; the prefix *e-*, which means out; and the suffix *-ate*, which means the act of. Therefore, to educate someone means to be engaged in the act of leading them out of ignorance. As I see it, education as it is currently presented in most classrooms in English-speaking countries does a fairly inadequate job of leading students out of ignorance. While we may do a fair to middling job of teaching maths and reading and spelling, some science, some social studies, and lots of computer technology, we often do a really poor job of educating students in the areas of self-control, responsibility, respect, empathy and creativity. These, I believe, are the qualities which we need to see in future generations if we are to be a successful society, to say nothing of becoming a civilised society.

So here are some of the techniques I have used in elementary and junior high classrooms in order to create an environment which encourages the development of the aforementioned qualities.

Dr James Daughtery of Drake University taught me that 60 per cent of what we learn comes to us through our ears. Fact. Therefore, to enhance learning of subject matter and a sense of responsibility for one's own learning, the first thing students see when they enter my classroom is a large poster on which are listed the following listening skills:

1. Good listeners have quiet hands, feet and mouths. (Eliminates gum chewing, talking and whispering inappropriately, writing notes, picking noses, fiddling around with a variety of things.)
2. Good listeners keep their eyes on the person who is speaking. (Eliminates daydreaming, wool-gathering, window-gazing, ignoring whoever is speaking.)
3. Good listeners listen from the beginning to the very end. (Eliminates hand-waving and questions in the middle of what the speaker is saying. The question will probably be answered, if the listeners are willing to wait.)
4. Good listeners decide to learn something. (It is the job of the educator to lead the students out of ignorance; it is the job of the student to make the journey. The educator is responsible for providing the information and a secure learning environment; the student is responsible for her or his own learning.)

The parenthetical information is not included on the sign, but is included in the discussion of those rules, which are the most valuable information they will learn during the year. The true value of the listening skills becomes ever more obvious as the students learn faster than they ever have before. 'Sixty per cent of what we learn comes to us ...'

I didn't know how to teach reading, in spite of having passed all my elementary education course with flying colours, until I met Paula Rome, an amazing woman who was not a teacher but the founder and director of the Orton Dyslexia Learning Center in Rochester,

Minnesota. According to those who were knowledgeable in the area of reading differences, the vast majority of those students who are identified as having reading disabilities actually have dyslexia, a learning condition which requires that they be taught to read in a certain specific way. If you really believe in teaching every child to read, take a course in Orton-Gillingham Phonics and become the most successful educator in your school, city, state, country, or continent. Slight exaggeration? No, fact.

I didn't really become an educator until 1968 when, the day after Martin Luther King Jr was killed, I finally used the blue-eyed, brown-eyed exercise on discrimination in my classroom with 26 third grade nine year olds. Up until then, I had been obeying the advice of the college instructor who told us, 'When you start teaching, don't teach in opposition to the local mores; the people in the school district are paying your wages through their taxes and they have the right to have their kids learn what they want them to.' Only when I watched my brown-eyed third-graders become me and the other significant adults in their environment as they treated the 'Blueys' the way we white folks have always treated coloured citizens, did I become aware of what real education could be. That day, I learned more than I taught, and more than I had ever learned in a college classroom. I truly led students out of ignorance on that day, and have never forgotten what they and I learned.

Now, you may be thinking, 'How dare you put little white third-graders through such an exercise? Don't you realise that you could do a child great psychological damage with that kind of experiment?' My question to you is, 'Don't you realise that we do great psychological damage to coloured kids as they are exposed to that same exercise, but based on skin colour, every day?' I think the professor who told us not to teach in opposition to the local mores was wrong, and that Kenneth Clark, noted child psychologist, was right, when he summed up the blue-eyed, brown-eyed exercise in this way: '... it is possible to educate and produce a class of human beings united by understanding, acceptance, and empathy.' I know that it is also possible to educate students to be responsible and cooperative citizens.

John Dewey said we learn by doing. I believe that Dr Daugherty, Paula Rome and Kenneth Clark would have agreed with him. I know that I do.

To find out more about the life and work of Jane Elliott, visit her website (www.janeelliott.com).

ABOUT THE AUTHORS

Jeremy Blackman, Alannah and Madeline Foundation

Jeremy Blackman is the Alannah and Madeline Foundation's Senior Cybersafety Specialist. His work focuses on issues surrounding social media, cyberbullying, educational technology and cybersafety resources, and ensuring the youth perspective is considered in industry initiatives. Jeremy has written about, presented and facilitated discussions on these topics across Australia, and was an ambassador for the Australian Internet Governance Forum in 2013.

The Alannah and Madeline Foundation, a national charity protecting children from violence and creating behavioural change in the community to address bullying and cyberbullying, became a Positive Schools partner in 2014.

Holly Brennan, Family Planning Queensland

Holly Brennan OAM is Director of Education and Community Services at Family Planning Queensland (FPQ). FPQ has been providing education, resources, training and information services to children, families, educators and other service providers for 40 years. Holly lives and works out of the Sunshine Coast and is the author and project coordinator of numerous resources and training packages, including FPQ's new book *Is this normal? Understanding your child's sexual behaviour*, which she co-authored with Judy Graham.

George W. Burns, Cairnmillar Institute

'We all want to be happy,' believes Professor George Burns, who has devoted his professional career to helping people achieve happiness. Recognised nationally and internationally for his innovative work in the area of happiness and wellbeing, George is an Adjunct Professor of Psychology, a clinical psychologist, prolific author and acclaimed trainer of therapists. George was invited to participate in a high-level United Nations meeting in 2012 on the need to address a nation's success in terms of wellbeing. He is also frequently invited to give keynote lectures, therapist training and workshops to international conferences and universities. George has published seven books, among them the much-acclaimed *Happiness, Healing, Enhancement* (2010), and is the author of more than 45 journal articles and book chapters.

He gives some of his time working as a volunteer clinical psychologist in poorer developing countries, and enjoys sharing his passions for nature, culture tales, and psychotherapy by leading colleagues on workshop/ study tours into areas such as the Himalayan kingdom of Bhutan – a country whose political philosophy and culture is based on Gross National Happiness.

Jane Burns, Young and Well Cooperative Research Centre

Associate Professor Jane Burns is the founder and CEO of the Young and Well Cooperative Research Centre. She holds a VicHealth Principal Research Fellowship at Orygen Youth Health Research Centre and an Honorary Fellowship at the Brain & Mind Research Institute. She has led the youth agenda for beyondblue and was a Commonwealth Fund Harkness Fellow at the University of California, San Francisco. She holds a PhD in Medicine from the University of Adelaide.

Jane was a Victorian Finalist in the 2012 Telstra Business Women's Awards and was listed in the *Financial Review* and Westpac Group 100 Women of Influence in 2012. Jane is an industrial girl at heart, having grown up in the lead smelting town of Port Pirie in South Australia. She is mum to three children, Angus, Holly and Harry, and juggles the demands of work and life by running ... everywhere. Her favourite app is RunKeeper and her life passion is driven by a desire to make the world a better place for her children. The Young and Well Cooperative Research Centre became a Positive Schools partner in 2014.

Michael Carr-Gregg, Psychologist and parenting expert

Positive Schools Ambassador since 2013, Dr Michael Carr-Gregg is one of Australia's highest profile psychologists. He works in private practice in Melbourne. He is a columnist for *Girlfriend* magazine and *Australian Doctor* and specialises in the area of parenting adolescents and adolescent mental health.

Michael has been the Consultant Psychologist to the Victorian Secondary Schools Principals Association, Australian Boarding Staff Association, Australian Ballet School, St Catherine's School, and Melbourne Girls' College. In 2003 he was one of the founding members of the National Coalition against Bullying and became one of their national spokespersons. Most importantly, Michael is married and has two children, supports Hawthorn in the AFL and South Sydney in the NRL.

Sandra Craig, Alannah and Madeline Foundation

Sandra Craig is manager of the National Centre Against Bullying (NCAB), an initiative of the Alannah and Madeline Foundation. NCAB is a peak body working to advise and inform the Australian community on the issue of childhood bullying and the creation of safe schools and communities. Sandra has worked on large-scale research and evaluation projects on school bullying and school attendance with Deakin and RMIT universities and recently contributed a chapter in *From Cyber Bullying to Cyber Safety: Issues and Approaches in Educational Contexts* (2013).

The Alannah and Madeline Foundation, a national charity protecting children from violence and creating behavioural change in the community to address bullying and cyberbullying, became a Positive Schools partner in 2014.

Julie Davey, A For Attitude

Julie Davey is dedicated to encouraging people to focus upon their strengths and reach their potential. Initially trained as a General Nurse (Division 1), and mindful of the influence of mindset and prevention (or early intervention) in the attainment of wellbeing, Julie has spent the past 20 years researching Positive Psychology and presenting relevant theories in resources suitably attractive to children. She encourages parents to communicate positive messages to their children from Day One.

Author of eight books distributed in 14 countries, she has presented to audiences in Singapore, New Zealand and Australia. Four of her books, including *The FabFirst5*, have been translated into Korean.

Maggie Dent

Maggie Dent is an author and educator specialising in parenting and resilience with a particular interest in the early years and adolescence. She is a passionate advocate for the healthy, common-sense raising of children in order to strengthen families and communities. She has a broad perspective and range of experience that shapes her work, a slightly irreverent sense of humour and a depth of knowledge based on modern research and ancient wisdom that she shares passionately in a common-sense way.

Maggie names her finest achievements as her four sons and a deep human connectedness.

Katherine Dix, Principals Australia Institute and Flinders University

Dr Katherine Dix is Senior Research Officer at Principals Australia Institute and an adjunct researcher at Flinders University. She has been Project Manager and chief analyst for both national evaluations of KidsMatter and their associated studies into children with disability. Dr Dix currently leads the innovative development of the online data management and quality monitoring interface that underpins the national rollout of KidsMatter.

KidsMatter and Principals Australia Institute have been key Positive Schools partners since 2011.

Jane Elliott

Jane Elliott, internationally known teacher, lecturer, diversity trainer and recipient of the US National Mental Health Association Award for Excellence in Education, exposes prejudice and bigotry for what it is, an irrational class system based upon purely arbitrary factors. And if you think this does not apply to you ... you are in for a rude awakening.

In response to the assassination of Martin Luther King Jr over thirty years ago, Jane Elliott devised the controversial and startling 'Blue Eyes/ Brown Eyes' exercise in her home town in Iowa, USA. This now famous exercise labels participants as inferior or superior based solely upon the colour of their eyes and exposes them to the experience of being a minority. Everyone who is exposed to Jane Elliott's work, be it through a lecture, workshop or video, is dramatically affected by it.

Andrew Fiu, LifeAfter6

Ta'afuli Andrew Fiu is author of the memoir *Purple Heart*, his account of growing up Samoan in New Zealand and of the four and a half years he spent in hospital coping with a serious heart condition (undergoing six open-heart surgeries) following a bout of rheumatic fever.

Purple Heart (Random House, 2006) is in study for NCEA exams and has been an English study text since 2007 in New Zealand. As its popularity among schools and colleges grew, Andrew's demand as a speaker and motivator nationwide increased. He is also in demand as a motivational speaker for big business, most recently in America and Singapore.

Andrew encourages students to develop their imagination and hold on to the belief that they can achieve their dreams, if they continue to learn.

Andrew Fuller

Andrew Fuller works with schools and communities in Australia and internationally, specialising in the wellbeing of young people and their families. He is a Fellow of the Department of Psychiatry and the Department of Learning and Educational Development at the University of Melbourne. In addition to several bestselling books, Andrew co-authored a series of programs for the promotion of resilience and emotional intelligence used in over 3500 schools in Britain and Australia. Andrew continues to counsel young people.

Andrew has recently been the scientific consultant for the ABC on a five-episode series, *Whatever: the science of the teenage brain*. He was a principal consultant to the national drug prevention strategy REDI, the ABC on children's television shows, is an Ambassador for MindMatters and is a member of the National Coalition Against Bullying. His most recent book, *Life: A Guide*, is available in bookshops. He is the author of *Tricky Kids*, now published in ten languages, and many other popular titles.

Dan Haesler, Happy Schools

Described as engaging, thought-provoking and someone who pushes the boundaries, Dan Haesler has appeared alongside some of the world's most respected educational thinkers, including Sir Ken Robinson, Stephen Heppell and Barbara Fredrickson. As well as speaking around Australia, Dan's work has featured in professional journals and the mainstream media. In 2012 he was quoted in the Australian Houses of Parliament during a Senate Debate on Youth Depression and Suicide. He also writes for the education page of the *Sydney Morning Herald*.

Dan works with schools, universities, corporate companies and not-for-profit organisations. He is the founder of YouthEngage, a not-for-profit initiative aimed at helping vulnerable kids to engage in learning and not get overlooked in the school system.

Steve Heron, Nurture Works

Steve Heron is founder of Nurture Works and developer of BUZ – Build Up Zone. Steve has over 35 years experience working in pastoral care with children in schools, families, camps and the community. Author of *BUZOLOGY: Powering Hope in Children* and *Bully Proofing: the Art of Social Confidence for Children*, Steve is also a children's book author, songwriter and an innovator in his field. He has been described as an affirmative vandal because of his positive approach to making the world a better place for children.

Steve is currently contracted by YouthCARE (Western Australia) to train chaplains and teachers in BUZ initiatives and programs in schools and has grassroots experience two days a week as a YouthCARE chaplain in a public school.

Dorothy Hoddinott, Holroyd High School

Dorothy Hoddinott is Principal of Holroyd High School in Sydney's western suburbs. Holroyd High is a Priority Schools Program school, and in 2011–12 took part in the low SES schools partnerships. The school builds high expectations for its students, of whom approximately 60 per cent are young refugees. Currently, over 40 per cent of students who complete their HSC at Holroyd High gain university entrance.

Dorothy has a deep commitment to social justice and has been a strong public advocate for the human rights of refugees and asylum seekers. In 2004, she was shortlisted for the Australian Human Rights Medal. She was conferred an Honorary Fellow of the University of Sydney in 2006, and in 2008 was made an Officer of the Order of Australia. She is a Fellow of the Australian College of Educators, and was awarded the College Medal in 2012, the first time the medal has been awarded to a practising school educator. She was appointed a Fellow of Senate of the University of Sydney in 2010.

Natalie Houghton, Jane Goodall Institute Australia

CEO of the Jane Goodall Institute Australia, Natalie has had a diverse and rich life: teaching Indigenous children in the Northern Territory, co-owning and managing sheep and cattle stations in outback Queensland, and running whale-watching eco-tourism adventures.

Natalie studied Animal Welfare through Monash University, where she discovered long-term solutions to animal welfare problems – Humane Education and Jane Goodall's global Roots & Shoots program. Natalie recognised the power of Humane Education in breaking the cycle of violence and apathy and creating change for a better world for animals, people and ecosystems.

Natalie appreciates that to be compassionate, sustainable and peaceful Earth stewards, we need to make ethical choices every day, and to make these ethical choices, we need knowledge. We need to unveil secrets, expose truths and empower ourselves to live in alignment with our values.

The Jane Goodall Institute is a global conservation and humanitarian organisation with offices in 26 countries around the world. Visit their Australian website at www.janegoodall.org.au.

John Irvine, Dr John's Happy Families

Dr John Irvine is one of Australia's most heard, seen and read child psychologist. He had his own one-teacher school at the age of 18, then taught in NSW schools for several years before becoming a child psychologist. He was awarded the Shell Prize for Arts and the University Medal during his studies at the University of New England. Dr John initiated preschool training in Toowoomba at the University of Southern Queensland where he also set up the state's first and most comprehensive family day care and family support scheme and has a community house dedicated to his name for services rendered to families in the region.

John is a regular guest on current affairs and news TV spots and has appeared weekly on Channel Ten's *9am with David and Kim*. He writes for several newspapers and has a radio segment, *Coping With Kids,* airing on many radio stations across Australia. He is a sought-after speaker around the nation and is proud to be patron of Family Day Care, Home Start, NAPCAN and Kidsafe and an ambassador for Playgroups. Dr John is a consultant child psychologist at the READ clinic, which he and his brother Warwick initiated in Gosford (www.drjohnshappyfamilies.com.au). Dr John has written several books, including *Who'd be a Parent*, *A Handbook for Happy Families* and *Thriving at School.*

Andrew J. Martin, University of Sydney

Professor Andrew Martin is a Registered Psychologist, Member of the College of Developmental and Educational Psychologists, and President-Elect of Division 5 (Educational, Instructional, and School Psychology) of the International Association of Applied Psychology. His research is focused on motivation, engagement and achievement; boys' and girls' education; gifted and talented education; disengagement; academic buoyancy and courage; pedagogy; parenting; teacher–student relationships and Aboriginal education. Andrew was listed in *Bulletin* magazine's SMART 100 Australians and in the Top 10 in the field of Education. His books, *How to Motivate Your Child For School and Beyond* (Bantam, 2003) and *How to Help Your Child Fly Through Life: The 20 Big Issues* (Bantam, 2005), are published in five languages and have been enthusiastically received by schools and parents across Australia and beyond. His latest book is *Building Classroom Success: Eliminating academic fear and failure* (Continuum, 2010).

Toni Noble, National Safe Schools Framework

Professor Toni Noble is a leading educator and psychologist working in the fields of children's and young people's wellbeing and positive school communities. Her Australian government projects include National Safe Schools Framework, the new Safe Schools Hub and the Scoping Study on Student Wellbeing. She is a co-author of the award-winning *BounceBack!* (a wellbeing and resilience program); *HITS & HOTS* (on student engagement), and *Eight Ways at Once* (on curriculum differentiation) and other books. Toni is Adjunct Professor in the Faculty of Education at Australian Catholic University and on the Advisory Board for the National Centre Against Bullying. Toni has been a Positive Schools Conference Ambassador since 2013.

Richard Pengelley, Christ Church Grammar School

The Reverend Richard Pengelley is the Director of Service Learning and Leadership and the Assistant Chaplain at Christ Church Grammar School in Western Australia.

Richard was born in Bahrain and came to Australia as a ten-pound Pom. Educated in Perth, he graduated from UWA as a PE teacher in 1981. After working in state schools he accepted a job at Hale School where he eventually became the Chaplain and an ordained Anglican priest. He has since run a large parish, been a university college Chaplain, Assistant Professor in Sports Science and Sub-Dean UWA Community. He chairs the boards of two NGOs: True Blue Dreaming, which provides mentors for educationally underprivileged WA school children, and Special Olympics WA, which provides sport and social opportunities for intellectually disabled Western Australians.

Richard is a member of the Positive Schools Conference team and has hosted the WA event in previous years as well as presenting on the main stage. Richard is a dual Olympian and captain of the Australian water polo team. He is married to a teacher with whom he has three adult daughters, two of whom are also teachers. His passions include sport, the beach, reading, travel and boys' and men's spiritual and emotional health.

Neil Porter

With a broad background in technology, psychology and law, Neil Porter brings a unique blend of skills and expertise to his role as founding member and co-chair of The National Australian Positive Schools Initiative. Neil has been instrumental in ensuring the Positive Schools conferences continually highlight the most important ideas and strategies in Positive Education and bring those ideas and strategies to an increasingly wide audience.

In addition to his role as co-chair of the conferences, Neil is co-founder of *The Positive Times* online magazine for educators, and director of Wise Solutions mental health assessment services for schools. These projects have ensured that advances in school-based wellbeing have been accessed by more than 10,000 schools worldwide. Neil is particularly interested in the development of effective platforms for distributing mental health information to teachers, the application of technology to Positive Education and the need for schools to better understand the role of wellbeing in academic learning.

Principals Australia Institute – KidsMatter Primary

Principals Australia Institute's (PAI) programs and services help build effective, inspirational and sustainable leadership in Australia's 10,000 government, Catholic and independent primary and secondary schools. PAI has been involved in leading the implementation of two national initiatives in schools: KidsMatter Primary and MindMatters.

KidsMatter Primary is a mental health and wellbeing initiative for Australian primary schools. It is a flexible, whole-school approach that provides schools with proven methods, resources and support to help children flourish and learn. More than 1,400 schools around Australia are implementing the initiative. KidsMatter Primary has been developed in collaboration with the Principals Australia Institute, the Australian Psychological Society and beyondblue, with funding from the Australian Government Department of Health and Ageing and beyondblue.

KidsMatter and Principals Australia Institute have been key Positive Schools partners since 2011.

Justin Robinson, Geelong Grammar School

Justin Robinson is Head of Positive Education at Geelong Grammar School. His role involves strategically shaping the direction of Positive Education across Geelong Grammar School's four campuses. This includes the explicit teaching of Positive Psychology to students in Years 7, 8,

9 and 10. Prior to this, Justin was the Head of Allen House, a senior co-educational day boarding house. Justin has a Master of Education (Policy and Administration) from Monash University.

Geelong Grammar School has been implementing the principles of Positive Education since 2008, when Martin Seligman came and trained staff in the tenets of Positive Psychology. Visit the school's website (www.ggs.vic.edu.au) to gain a deeper understanding of the school and their Model for Positive Education.

Geelong Grammar School has been a key Positive Schools partner since 2013.

Sue Roffey, Wellbeing Australia

Dr Sue Roffey is Adjunct Associate Professor at the University of Western Sydney, founder and Director of Wellbeing Australia and Fellow of the UK Royal Society of Arts (RSA). She is also Lead Co-Convenor of the Student Wellbeing Action Network and Director of NAPCAN's Aboriginal Girls Circle initiative. She developed Circle Solutions for Student Wellbeing (Sage, 2014), a philosophy and pedagogy for social and emotional learning (see www.circlesolutionsnetwork.com/csn).

Sue lives between Sydney and London and is an international authority on issues related to behaviour in school, social and emotional learning, relational quality and wellbeing in education. She is a prolific author of books and journal articles on these issues, and an inspiring speaker and advocate for the authentic wellbeing of children and communities.Sue is the founder and a director of Wellbeing Australia. To find out more about Wellbeing Australia visit www.wellbeingaustralia.com.au/wba.

Tim Sharp 'Dr Happy', The Happiness Institute

Professor Tim Sharp is an expert in human behaviour and thinking. He knows that understanding and connecting with people (including getting the most out of them) is a serious business. Tim takes it so seriously that he is passionate about making it fun and entertaining so his audiences actually listen and learn. Tim has three degrees in psychology, and more than two decades experience as a clinical psychologist, executive coach, corporate consultant, entrepreneur, manager, employer and parent.

Tim is widely regarded as one of the world's leading experts in the field of positive psychology and is highly regarded among his academic colleagues (holding professorial appointments at UTS Business School and RMIT School of Health Sciences) as well as those in the business community. He is a bestselling author and regular media commentator who's been read and heard and seen by literally millions of people over the last few years via his appearances on TV and radio and contributions to the *Australian Financial Review*, *Sydney Morning Herald*, *Sun Herald* and *Sunday Telegraph*.

Helen Street, National Australian Positive Schools Initiative and University of Western Australia

Social psychologist, author and educator Dr Helen Street has worked extensively in Australian schools since 1999. Her work focuses on positive education, wellbeing, goal setting and motivation and has been presented internationally in academic journals and in the popular media. Helen's work has met with international acclaim and has been endorsed by His Holiness the Dalai Lama and 'Blue Eyes/Brown Eyes' creator Jane Elliott, among many others. In addition to her academic role, Helen is an adjunct research consultant for the health department of WA's Centre for Clinical Interventions and co-chair for the Positive Schools conferences. In 2011 Helen was awarded the title of Honorary Research Fellow with the School of Graduate Education at UWA. She has been a regular guest psychologist for Channel Ten and is now a regular feature writer for the *Western Teacher*. As well as being one of the original creators of Positive Schools, Helen is a regular host and presenter at the events and one of the co-founders of *The Positive Times* (www.positivetimes.com.au), a free online magazine for educators.

Helen founded and co-chaired the Positive Schools mental health and wellbeing conferences (www.positiveschools.com.au) with Neil Porter in 2009. Her books include *Standing Without Shoes* (2003) written with George Burns and *Life Overload* (2011). Visit her website (www.helenstreet. com.au) to find out more.

Melinda Tankard Reist, Collective Shout

Melinda Tankard Reist is a Canberra author, speaker, media commentator, blogger and advocate for women and girls. Her third book, *Getting Real: Challenging the Sexualisation of Girls* (Spinifex Press, 2009), is now in its fourth printing. *Big Porn Inc: Exposing the harms of the global pornography industry*, co-edited with Dr Abigail Bray, is also published by Spinifex Press (2011).

Melinda is a regular guest on Channel 7's *The Morning Show*, and has also appeared on ABC's *Q&A* and *The Gruen Sessions* as well as a number of other TV and radio programs. She is a regular contributor to ABC's *The Drum Unleashed*, and other online opinion sites.

Two years ago Melinda initiated a grassroots campaigning movement – Collective Shout: for a world free of sexploitation – to expose corporations, advertisers and marketers who objectify women and sexualise girls to sell products and services. Collective Shout has achieved significant wins against major companies in a short time.

Visit Collective Shout at www.collectiveshout.org to support her ongoing initiative to create a healthier online world for young people with regard to sex and relationships.

Mathew White, St Peter's College

Dr Mathew White is Director of Wellbeing at the independent boys school St Peter's College, Adelaide, where he serves on the school's Senior Leadership Team. He obtained his PhD from the University of Adelaide and completed residential studies at Harvard's Graduate School of Education. Mathew is a Fellow at the Melbourne Graduate School of Education and a Research Affiliate of the Well-being Institute at Cambridge University.

As an academic, Mathew has authored chapters and peer-reviewed articles on leadership, cultural change, wellbeing and positive psychology. He has advised corporate, non-profit, government and Catholic education systems on positive psychology applications including the Executive Service program in the Department of Premier and Cabinet. Mathew was one of sixteen invited speakers at the inaugural Positive Education Summit at 10 Downing Street in October 2013 and Wellington College, Berkshire. He has senior experience in strategic planning, relationship management, communications and organisational change. He was a member of the start-up team at Teach for Australia, an independent, social enterprise addressing educational disadvantage. Mathew taught at Geelong Grammar School where he held positions of academic and pastoral responsibility for eleven years and was the first Head of Positive Education.

First published 2014 by
FREMANTLE PRESS
25 Quarry Street, Fremantle 6160
(PO Box 158, North Fremantle 6159)
Western Australia
www.fremantlepress.com.au

Also available as an ebook.

Cover photograph © iStock.
Printed by Everbest Printing Company, China

National Library of Australia Cataloguing-in-Publication entry
Better than OK : helping young people to flourish at school and beyond / edited by
    Dr Helen Street and Neil Porter.
ISBN: 9781922089793 (paperback), 9781922089809 (ebook)
Notes: Includes bibliographical references and index.
Subjects: Youth—Life skills guides.
    Youth—Conduct of life.
    Study skills.
    Self-actualization (Psychology)
    Youth development.
Other Authors/Contributors:
    Street, Helen, 1966– editor.
    Porter, Neil, editor.
Dewey Number: 305.2355

Government of **Western Australia**
Department of **Culture and the Arts**

Fremantle Press is supported by the State Government through the Department of Culture and the Arts.